DAIMLER FLEETLINE

GAVIN BOOTH

Ian Allan
PUBLISHING

Contents

	Foreword	3
1	Before the Fleetline	4
2	The first Fleetlines	12
3	All change for Daimler ?	34
4	London tries the Fleetline	46
5	Export success	50
6	Success in the new era	54
7	The Fleetline in figures	70
8	Bodying the Fleetline	74
9	After the Fleetline	82
10	Fleetlines in later life	86
11	Evaluating the Fleetline	92
	Appendix: Fleetline customers	94
	Bibliography	96

Front cover: **BET-group companies were enthusiastic customers for the Daimler Fleetline, some, like Yorkshire Woollen, buying both Fleetlines and Leyland Atlanteans in the 1960s. This 1971 CRG6LX Fleetline with 75-seat Alexander body is seen leaving Dewsbury bus station.** Dale Tringham

Back cover (upper): **London Transport eventually accounted for nearly a quarter of all Fleetline sales, though its experience with the type was not always happy. A 1976 CRL6 with 71-seat Metro-Cammell body is seen at Chipstead Valley.** Mark Page

Back cover (lower): **The Fleetline enjoyed some success with independent operators. In 1978 Leon, Finningley, bought this FE30AGR with 75-seat Northern Counties body, one of five Fleetlines bought new. It is seen in Doncaster.** H. J. Black

Previous page: **In 1965 Bournemouth Corporation took 10 convertible open-top Fleetlines with 74-seat Weymann bodywork, one of which is seen here at Boscombe. In 1977 seven of these buses, including this one, passed to London Transport for sightseeing work.** Tony Wilson

First published 2010

ISBN 978 0 7110 3456 3

All rights reserved. No part of this book may be reproduced or transmitted in any form or by any means, electronic or mechanical, including photocopying, recording or by any information storage and retrieval system, without permission from the Publisher in writing.

© Ian Allan Publishing Ltd 2010

Published by Ian Allan Publishing

an imprint of Ian Allan Publishing Ltd, Hersham, Surrey, KT12 4RG
Printed in England by Ian Allan Printing Ltd, Hersham, Surrey, KT12 4RG

Code: 1008/B2

Distributed in the United States of America and Canada by BookMasters Distribution Services

Visit the Ian Allan Publishing website at www.ianallanpublishing.com

Foreword

Daimler's shrewd assessment in the late 1950s of the future needs of the double-deck bus market produced a chassis that was a success by any measure. The Fleetline combined the rear-engined layout of Leyland's Atlantean with a genuine low-height capability and the respected Gardner engine in a chassis that would surpass its maker's expectations by selling to a much wider audience than it could have dared to hope for. Daimler's traditional customer base had been the UK's municipal bus fleets, yet the Fleetline took Daimlers into company-owned, state-owned and independent fleets, achieved impressive export sales and even managed to break into London Transport.

The Fleetline also survived the massive changes to the industry at the end of the 1960s that created the PTEs and National Bus Company and potentially robbed Daimler of faithful customers; and there were the changes of ownership that brought Daimler into the British Leyland fold along with its closest rival, the Leyland Atlantean, and the relatively recent Bristol VRT. Both were obvious rivals, particularly as the VRT offered a Gardner engine and a proper low-height capability. But sales of the Atlantean, Fleetline and VRT were buoyed by the demise of traditional front-engined double-deck chassis that was sparked by the introduction of New Bus Grant, which encouraged operators to stock up with models suitable for what was the still known as one-man operation.

In the 1970s the future of all of Leyland's double-deck models was threatened by a move to a single new model, the Titan, but operator resistance to this highly standardised and sophisticated integral design ensured that the older chassis survived into the 1980s — though only just, as far as the Fleetline and VRT were concerned; production stopped in 1980 and 1981 respectively, while the Atlantean, which had been upgraded in 1972 as the improved AN68 series, remained available in the UK until 1984 — and for export markets until 1986.

By this time there were newcomers to the double-deck scene, including some, like the Dennis Dominator and MCW Metrobus, that offered Gardner engines and low-height options, although Leyland's real all-purpose double-deck replacement, the Olympian, was by far the most successful.

Only London seemed to have real problems with the Fleetline, and London's problems resulted in an invaluable stream of used double-deckers appearing on the market — both in the UK and overseas — at a time when operators were desperate to get hold of decent buses for one-man-operated services.

The Fleetline deserves its place as one of the most successful and most highly regarded double-deck models of all time. This book, timed to coincide with the 50th anniversary of its introduction, is a tribute to the people who designed, built and operated it.

Gavin Booth
Edinburgh
July 2010

Darlington Corporation was an enthusiastic Daimler customer, moving from CCG5 double-deckers to Roadliners — perhaps less enthusiastically — and quickly to Fleetline single-deckers. Darlington bought no new Fleetline double-deckers. Seen in the town centre, with a Roe-bodied CCG5 in the background, is one of 12 Fleetline SRG6LX with 48-seat two-door Marshall bodywork delivered in 1970. Tony Wilson

Before the Fleetline

The Fleetline represented a last triumphant flourish for Daimler, a fitting reminder of a proud British company.

Daimler's origins are associated with what became the giant Daimler-Benz business, but while Gottlieb Daimler designed and produced some of the most effective early motor-car engines, the Daimler company in Britain was set up by Frederick Richard Simms, who had bought the exclusive patent rights for the Daimler engine in the UK. He formed the Daimler Motor Syndicate Ltd in London in 1893 and the Daimler Motor Co Ltd, with its base in Coventry, in 1896. The latter would shortly become the Daimler Company Ltd under the ownership of the Birmingham Small Arms Co Ltd.

Daimler was essentially a builder of quality cars, but as early as 1908 it had produced an advanced petrol-electric integral steel-built double-deck model and in 1912 had won a substantial order for double-deckers for London. This led in the same year to its first links with AEC, at this time part of the Underground group, and Daimler became selling agents for AEC models that were surplus to AEC requirements. A closer relationship was formed with AEC in 1926 when the Associated Daimler Company (ADC) was created to market and sell AEC and Daimler bus and commercial chassis; ADC lasted until 1929, when AEC and Daimler went their separate ways.

Success in the bus market for Daimler really came in the 1930s. Following a series of unsuccessful attempts to offer late-model petrol engines in its chassis, it was the adoption of the fluid flywheel and Wilson preselector epicyclic gearbox, (first in Daimler cars and from 1931 in bus chassis) and Gardner 5LW and 6LW diesel engines (from 1934) that really secured Daimler's place among the major players in the British bus market.

The engines and gearboxes were not unique to Daimler. London General had bought three Daimler CH6 models with preselector 'boxes in 1931 and moved increasingly towards preselector gearboxes on its new full-sized buses, but these were AECs and Leylands rather than Daimlers.

Daimler won a substantial order for London buses in 1912, and more than 200 were supplied to Tramways (MET) from 1913. Daimler Y types were among the many London buses sent to France and Belgium as troop-carriers during the Great War, as seen here.
Author's collection

The Daimler COG5 was particularly associated with urban duties, but some received coach bodywork, among them this 1935 Roberts-bodied example for Bowen, Musselburgh. Author's collection

Various chassis builders, notably Bristol and Guy, offered Gardner engines, but coupled to less driver-friendly gearboxes. Bus operators still had a fairly wide choice in the 1930s, so Daimler was competing for orders with big hitters like AEC and Leyland as well as with smaller companies, notably Albion, Bristol and Crossley, that had faithful, often local customers.

Playing the local card was important to municipal bus operators, and there were just under 100 of these corporation fleets in the 1930s. Buses with locally built chassis and/or bodies supported the economy, and many transport committees strove to order their buses with at least some local content. With its production based in Coventry, Daimler saw the West Midlands as an obvious target area, though Guy, based at Wolverhampton, was nibbling at the edges and would establish itself more firmly in the 1940s. AEC and Leyland already had a foothold in Birmingham, but this would be where Daimler achieved its greatest prewar success, Birmingham City Transport buying more than 800 COG5 double-deckers and single-deckers between 1934 and 1939. Outside London, which was firmly wedded to AEC but took batches of Leylands to maintain some sense of balance, Birmingham was the biggest urban bus fleet, with some 800 buses in 1938.

The Daimler CO — be it in COG5 form with 7.0-litre Gardner 5LW engine or COG6 with 8.4-litre Gardner 6LW for the likes of Edinburgh, where extra power was needed to tackle hills — was a popular urban bus, drivers appreciating

the ease of control offered by the preselector gearbox. Although most models had Gardner engines the Coventry municipal fleet specified the AEC 7.7-litre engine, resulting in the COA6.

During World War 2 Daimler was one of the nominated suppliers of utility double-deck chassis, but as the Daimler factory had been badly damaged in the air raids on Coventry in 1940/1 wartime production was based at Wolverhampton. The first 100 chassis were CWG5 models, with the Gardner 5LW engine, but CWA6, with AEC's 7.7-litre A173, became standard. Both retained the preselective gearbox, so the wartime chassis were broadly similar to the prewar CO range.

Daimler was keen to offer its own engines, as AEC and Leyland did, and had been working on what in 1944 became the 8.6-litre CD6; this was fitted to some utility chassis designated CWD6. In total Daimler built more than 1,500 CW-series chassis between 1942 and 1947.

Daimler's postwar standard models followed the established and successful combination of a Gardner engine driving through a preselector gearbox, though the company did try to push its CD6 unit, fitted to the CVD6 model. The 'V' stood for Victory, and there were also CVA6 (AEC-engined) CVG5 and CVG6 (Gardner-engined) models. Birmingham chose the CVA6, CVD6 and CVG6 types as part of its postwar restocking, though it also bought AECs, Crossleys, Guys and Leylands to get buses in the quantities it required.

In the postwar years Daimler achieved

THE BEST BUS CHASSIS IN THE WORLD

★ INCORPORATING EVERY KNOWN ENGINEERING IMPROVEMENT

★ **FLUID FLYWHEEL TRANSMISSION**
THE ONLY KNOWN SYSTEM WHICH HAS A FLUID DRIVE ON TOP GEAR

★ **AUTOMATIC CHASSIS LUBRICATION**

★ **AUTOMATICALLY ADJUSTED DEWANDRE LOCKHEED BRAKES**

★ **GARDNER ENGINE, DAIMLER FLOAT MOUNTED**

★ **ELECTRIC CABLES, CARRIED IN METAL CONDUITS ON DASH, GIVING MAXIMUM PROTECTION**

TRANSPORT VEHICLES (DAIMLER) LIMITED, COVENTRY

Above: Daimler was no shrinking violet when it came to its advertising. 'The Best Bus Chassis in the World', the COG family — this is a COG5 — was the range that really cemented Daimler's position as a leading bus-chassis builder. This advertisement appeared in the trade press during 1938. Author's collection

Right: The COG range helped to sell Daimler chassis into export markets, and this 1938 trade-press advertisement shows recent South African and Australian deliveries. Author's collection

SOUTH AFRICA

More Daimler buses have recently been ordered for service in CAPETOWN, DURBAN, PIETERMARITZBURG and SPRINGS. The illustration shows a Daimler Double Deck bus passing through the centre of England en route for shipment to DURBAN.

THE BEST BUS CHASSIS IN THE WORLD

AUSTRALIA

Below is illustrated one of the Daimler buses ordered by United Buses Limited, leaving the Daimler Works for delivery to Perth, Australia. Other recent overseas orders for Daimler include chassis for NEW ZEALAND and SHANGHAI.

TRANSPORT VEHICLES (DAIMLER) LIMITED. COVENTRY

impressive double-deck sales in the British market, and in the period 1946-55 these amounted to some 3,391 chassis — more than Guy (1,946) and almost matching Bristol (3,517) but considerably fewer than AEC (8,486) or Leyland (8,706).

Daimler's tried and tested range was appreciated by the many municipal operators that kept coming back with repeat orders. In the early 1950s the company had followed the trend to underfloor-engined single-deck chassis by introducing the Freeline, but this heavyweight model never achieved the success of its AEC and Leyland rivals. Daimler also tested the market with an advanced double-decker, the CD650, fitted with a more powerful Daimler engine displacing 10.6 litres (or 650cu in, hence the model name). The chassis featured hydraulic brakes and power-assisted steering but was generally considered to be ahead of its time, and only 14 were delivered to British operators.

Although Daimler appeared to be happy producing well-made, traditionally engineered double-deckers it was not oblivious to developments elsewhere in the British bus-manufacturing industry. In the 1950s there were various obsessions — weight-saving to reduce

fuel, increasing seating capacity within the legal dimensions, and achieving a low overall height for double-deckers without resorting to the awkward 'lowbridge' layout, with sunken side gangway on the upper deck.

Daimler moved with the times with 30ft-long models when these were legalised in 1956. The main model was designated CVG6-30 (or from 1958 CVG6LX-30 with Gardner's 10.45-litre 6LX engine), but there was also a CVD650-30 variant with the 10.6-litre engine from the earlier CD650 model.

In 1957 the company introduced its direct-selection Daimatic gearbox with two-pedal control, and this, with the Gardner 6LX engine, became a popular choice for its front-engined double-deckers and would become the chosen powertrain for the next generation of model from Coventry. Meanwhile, in 1958, Daimler offered an alternative to the epicyclic gearboxes that had been fitted as standard to its bus chassis for more than 25 years; a David Brown synchromesh 'box became an option, resulting in the CSG5 and CSG6 models. In 1963, with Daimler and Guy under common Jaguar ownership, the CCG5 and CCG6 were offered with the Guy constant-mesh 'box.

At the 1957 Scottish Motor Show Daimler introduced the Daimatic semi-automatic gearbox, and this was fitted to Glasgow Corporation D217, a CVD650-30 with Alexander bodywork, which also introduced this style of glassfibre front end. The bus later received a Gardner 6LW engine in place of its original Daimler CD650 unit. Author's collection

A number of operators went for the 30ft-long Daimler CVG6-30 with forward-entrance bodywork. This is a 1967 Swindon Corporation example with 70-seat Northern Counties body. From 1968 Swindon turned to Fleetlines. Author's collection

Daimler had tried to address the weight problem with the CLG5, a pared-down CVG5, but only two appear to have been built. For years the onus was on bodybuilders to achieve maximum seating capacity within legal weight limits. In a 27ft-long double-decker 66 proved to be the maximum, but the increase to 30ft-long two-axle double-deckers allowed an extra row of seats on each deck, taking capacity to 74 (or 76 at a pinch on some models); any further increase would require the engine to be re-sited.

Leyland had been looking at rear-engined buses since the 1930s, culminating in the launch, at the 1956 Commercial Motor Show, of the Atlantean. Here was a proper low-height (13ft 3in) 78-seat double-decker, and for many this seemed to be the way forward. However, operators were unhappy with the Atlantean in its 1956 form — an integral bus with Metro-Cammell bodywork. This caused Leyland to rethink the Atlantean as a chassis — one that lacked the drop-centre rear axle of the prototype, which meant that it could not be a true low-height bus; Leyland expected full-height Atlanteans to be the main sellers but produced a compromise 'semi-lowbridge' version to cater for operators requiring lower buses. These had a rather awkward upper-deck layout with the rearmost four rows of seats

configured as on a lowbridge bus, with nearside side gangway and four-abreast seating. In the absence of a proper low-height rear-engined double-decker some operators were prepared to specify this version, but most Atlantean sales were to operators looking for a normal-height bus. With its change of approach, Leyland had unwittingly opened up an opportunity for Daimler.

Northampton Corporation stuck with the Roe-bodied rear-entrance Daimler CVG6 right to the end of home-market production in 1968. This is a 1967 delivery, among the last in a long line of Roe-bodied Daimlers for the undertaking. The final Northampton deliveries were also the last Daimler chassis fitted with preselective gearboxes. *Tony Wilson*

Below: The last front-engined Daimler bus chassis were CVG6LX models for Kowloon Motor Bus, Hong Kong, seen under construction at Daimler's Radford works in Coventry in 1970. *Author's collection*

The first Fleetlines

Given that Leyland had been actively developing what would become the Atlantean since the early 1950s, and even allowing for the fact that it had hastily rethought the concept between the 1956 prototype and the 1958 production chassis, Daimler had a lot of catching up to do. Rather than reinvent the breed, Daimler sensibly went for a layout similar to the Atlantean's, with a transversely mounted engine in a separate compartment at the rear. It also matched the Atlantean's 16ft 3in wheelbase, to make life easier for bodybuilders. But Daimler also made some significant changes that would greatly increase the appeal of its new model. Most notably, it went for a drop-centre rear axle, which meant that the lower-deck gangway could be flat, and this allowed a proper low-height bus with normal seating on both decks — something Leyland could not offer. It also mounted the Daimatic gearbox separately from the engine, reducing the build-up of heat that caused problems on early Atlanteans.

Daimler launched its new rear-engined double-deck bus chassis, the Fleetline, at the 1960 Commercial Show at Earl's Court, just two years after the first production Atlanteans had appeared, but although Leyland had a head start, only 600-odd Atlanteans were in service, so Daimler stood a chance of catching up.

Two buses were shown at Earl's Court — one a chassis, the other a Weymann-bodied demonstrator. These were introduced as RE30 models, a change from Daimler's previous type designations, which included details of the engine make. 'RE' stood for rear-engined, while '30' indicated the 30ft overall length. Following the basic layout established by Leyland's Atlantean, both had the engine — in this case Daimler's own 8.6-litre CD6 — mounted transversely across the rear, the engine being to the nearside and the Daimatic four-speed semi-automatic epicyclic gearbox on the offside. The 16ft 3in wheelbase also matched that of the Atlantean, but the major difference lay in the drop-centre rear axle, which allowed proper low-height bodywork if desired.

Contemporary Daimler brochures highlighted other important differences: 'The power unit is mounted transversely across the rear of

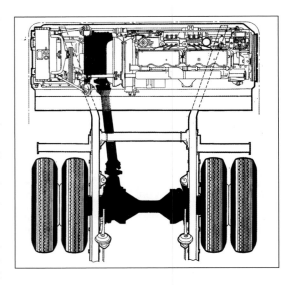

the chassis and, with the combined gearbox and right-angle-drive unit, is partly carried on a detachable subframe bolted to a substantial rear cross-member which carries the remainder of the power unit. Of special interest is the fact that individual units can be removed without disturbing the rest of the installation. … In unit with the engine is the high-efficiency Daimler fluid flywheel and Daimatic 4-speed epicyclic gearbox which also incorporates the right-angle drive to the dropped axle. This layout completely eliminates the need for a separate angle-drive unit and is a feature to be found only on the Fleetline chassis.' What Daimler did not get quite right was the choice of engine, but, as we shall see, this was quickly resolved. Although there would prove to be some weak points in the design, most operators were able to live with these because of the overall reliability and fuel efficiency.

The RE30 designation was quickly dropped, and the Fleetline was identified by designations that continued Daimler's traditions, the most common being the CRG6LX, indicating that the recently introduced 150bhp Gardner 10.45-litre 6LX engine had become the standard engine and that Daimler recognised that there was no real future for its CD6 unit. Gardner engines, beloved of engineers and accountants because of their reliability and fuel economy, were popular with many operators, while Leyland only offered its own engine in the Atlantean.

The bodied bus at the 1960 show was 7000 HP, a CRD6 demonstrator painted in Birmingham City Transport colours — partly, no doubt, because of the West Midlands connection but more significantly because Birmingham was a target customer. The Daimler marketing people had done their crystal-ball-gazing as the Fleetline was conceived and looked at Daimler's current customers and their likely attitude towards the new bus. London Transport was probably a long shot because it was firmly wedded to AEC and Leyland and was still taking deliveries of its front-engined Routemaster model (and indeed would continue to do so until 1968). Birmingham, on the other hand, was approaching the stage where it would need new buses. It had bought large batches of its standard double-deck type between 1947 and

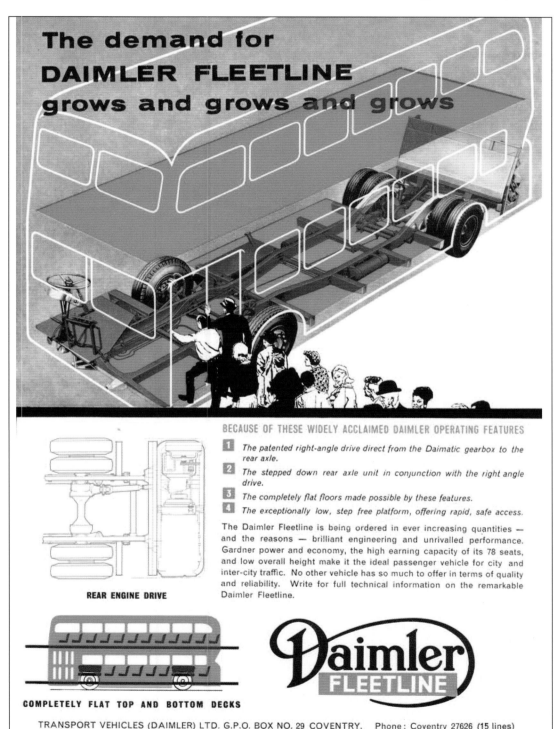

The demand for
DAIMLER FLEETLINE
grows and grows and grows

BECAUSE OF THESE WIDELY ACCLAIMED DAIMLER OPERATING FEATURES

1 The patented right-angle drive direct from the Daimatic gearbox to the rear axle.

2 The stepped down rear axle unit in conjunction with the right angle drive.

3 The completely flat floors made possible by these features.

4 The exceptionally low, step free platform, offering rapid, safe access.

The Daimler Fleetline is being ordered in ever increasing quantities — and the reasons — brilliant engineering and unrivalled performance. Gardner power and economy, the high earning capacity of its 78 seats, and low overall height make it the ideal passenger vehicle for city and inter-city traffic. No other vehicle has so much to offer in terms of quality and reliability. Write for full technical information on the remarkable Daimler Fleetline.

REAR ENGINE DRIVE

COMPLETELY FLAT TOP AND BOTTOM DECKS

Daimler FLEETLINE

TRANSPORT VEHICLES (DAIMLER) LTD. G.P.O. BOX NO. 29 COVENTRY.   Phone : Coventry 27626 (15 lines)

Far left and left: Two of the main differences between the Fleetline and Leyland's 1958-introduced Atlantean were the right-angle drive from the gearbox to the rear axle and the drop-centre rear axle, which allowed a flat gangway on both decks within the low-height dimensions. The right-angle drive is also shown in the smaller illustration. *Author's collection*

1954, following which the only additions to the fleet had been two ex-demonstrator AEC Bridgemasters. But more than half of the postwar Standards were Daimlers, and, with the oldest of these buses now 13 years old, Daimler must have thought it had a good chance.

Manchester was another municipal target, with a recent history of buying Daimlers alongside Leylands. Glasgow too seemed to like Daimlers but also bought AECs and Leylands. Liverpool had bought Daimlers in the postwar period but had stopped in 1950, preferring to dual-source AECs and Leylands. There were other municipal fleets that had kept their options open, among them Leeds, which had bought AEC, Daimler and Leyland double-deckers through the 1950s, and Sheffield, which had concentrated on AECs and Leylands. All of these big fleets were targets for the Fleetline, but Daimler was looking beyond its traditional municipal customer base. The low-height layout would surely appeal to company fleets like those in the BET and Scottish groups, and some of the Fleetline's early successes would be with unexpected customers.

It took Daimler a couple of years to get its Fleetline ready for production, so the first production examples did not enter service until 1962. Birmingham was in there with an order for 10 — matched by an order for 10 Atlanteans.

The chassis of the Fleetline was similar to the Leyland Atlantean in layout, wheelbase and general dimensions, but its trump card was the drop-centre rear axle, clearly seen here, which allowed a flat lower-saloon floor and, as a result, low-height double-deck bodies with normal seating on the upper deck.
Author's collection

Daimler FLEETLINE

ONE BUS—TWO JOBS

INTER-CITY with **78 seats** FLAT FLOORS & CENTRAL GANGWAY **CITY**

13'6"

62D

14A CITY

● **ELIMINATES THE LOW BRIDGE PROBLEM** ● **DRIVER CONTROLLED DOORS**
● **OUTSTANDING ECONOMY** ● LOW MAINTENANCE COSTS ● REAR ENGINE (GARDNER) AND AUTO-BRAKE ADJUSTERS

TRANSPORT VEHICLES (DAIMLER) LTD., G.P.O. BOX No. 29 COVENTRY TEL: COVENTRY 27626 (15 lines)
Full technical information on request

Fleetline prototype 7000 HP, wearing its Birmingham City Transport colours, featured in early Daimler advertising for the new model, in this case emphasising its adaptability as a city or inter-urban bus. Although Daimler's main double-deck market had been municipal operators, it was keen to break into the company and independent sectors, where many firms looked for low-height buses — hence the 13ft 6in bridge. *Author's collection*

Independent operators were early customers — Blue Bus of Willington and A1 Service of Ardrossan received early Northern Counties-bodied Fleetlines — and in addition to the more predictable sales, like Salford and Sunderland, there were breakthroughs. Sheffield Corporation took three early examples, while BET's Potteries subsidiary took one.

Production built up gradually, and as early as 1964 it was actually outselling the Atlantean; indeed, in that year the Fleetline was the UK's best-selling double-deck model, the quantities involved — more than 400 chassis — taking Daimler's double-deck sales back to the heady days of the early 1950s. New customers appeared; some stayed, while others went back to their previous suppliers, but it was a real success story, particularly as the Fleetline quickly established a reputation for reliability and frugality in terms of fuel consumption.

Among the orders that must have caused some celebrations at Coventry in the Fleetline's early years were those placed by the municipal fleets at Birkenhead, Bournemouth, Bury, Middlesbrough, Nottingham and Warrington, BET-group subsidiaries Maidstone & District, Mexborough & Swinton, Midland Red, North Western, Trent and Tynemouth & District, and even the Scottish Bus Group, with a significant first order for Western SMT.

None of these fleets had any real history with Daimler. Birkenhead Transport had last bought Daimlers in 1950 and had standardised on Guys and Leylands; Bournemouth and Bury were staunch Leyland fans and bought Atlanteans before their first Fleetlines; Middlesbrough had bought Guys and some Dennis Lolines before switching to Fleetlines in 1962; Warrington had bought Fodens and Leylands in the 1950s.

Winning orders from BET subsidiaries was particularly important to Daimler, as most of these companies, with fleets generally dominated by AECs and Leylands, had no history of Daimlers, the exception being Trent, which had bought COG5 types in the 1930s. Maidstone & District was a very early customer for Leyland's Atlantean, so the Fleetline deliveries in 1963/4 — and over the next six years — were particularly sweet for Daimler. Midland Red was another important convert, particularly as it had traditionally built its own BMMO buses, augmented by some proprietary models. Between 1963 and 1971 it took more than 300 Fleetlines, and until 1966 these were entering service alongside new front-engined BMMO D9 double-deckers.

The Scottish Bus Group's conservative vehicle policy was a hard nut to crack, but the Fleetline was helped by the group's requirement for low-height buses, and once Western SMT had placed its first order for 1965 delivery, other group companies eventually followed; SBG never bought any new Leyland Atlanteans.

Fleetline chassis 60003 was bodied in 1962 by Northern Counties for Tailby & George (Blue Bus Services) of Willington, in which fleet it was joined by prototype 7000 HP. Mark Page

Above: In the 1950s Sunderland Corporation had standardised on Gardner-engined Daimlers and Guys, so it will have been a target customer for the Fleetline. It bought Fleetlines from 1962 with a distinctive style of Roe bodywork. This is a 1964 delivery.
Dale Tringham

Below: BET's Potteries company had bought batches of early Leyland Atlanteans with low-height 'semi-lowbridge' Weymann bodies but turned to the Fleetline as a more practical low-height bus. This Northern Counties-bodied 73-seat example, seen in Hanley, was one of a batch of 15 delivered in 1963. Mark Page

Warrington Corporation was a new customer for Daimler and bought Fleetlines between 1963 and 1973. This 1967 bus had 77-seat East Lancs bodywork.
Mark Page

Other early Fleetline customers had more of a history with Daimler. The corporation fleets at Belfast, Coventry, Derby, Dundee, Glasgow, Grimsby-Cleethorpes, Leeds, Manchester, Rochdale, SHMD and South Shields were all active Daimler customers (though most dual- or multi-sourced their bus orders), and most would continue to buy Fleetlines for some years. Only Glasgow, which received a solitary Fleetline in 1963, would resist the model's charms and go on to build up a substantial fleet of Atlanteans.

Daimler also sold the Fleetline to independent fleets, many of which would come back, often for just one or two buses, but it was all good business. Tailby & George of Willington, trading as Blue Bus Services, received Fleetline chassis 60003, 60000 being demonstrator 7000 HP, 60001 an experimental chassis, and 60002 a demonstration chassis that was never bodied. Daimler's system of numbering its chassis in a separate series for each type makes it easy to follow the Fleetline's fortunes, although from 1975, when the model was rebranded a Leyland, Fleetlines would get a bit lost in Leyland's single series of chassis numbers. Other early independent customers were A1, Ardrossan; AA, Ayr; Beckett, Bucknall; Burwell & District; Graham, Paisley; and McGill, Barrhead. Lancashire United Transport bought six Fleetlines in 1962 and went on to buy more than

50 examples while still an independent concern.

The earliest Fleetlines were 30ft-long chassis with a 16ft 3in wheelbase and had bodywork by Alexander, East Lancs, Metro-Cammell, Northern Counties, Park Royal, Roe or Weymann, though a few were bodied by Massey and Willowbrook, and the substantial orders for Belfast Corporation received MH Cars bodywork, as did two examples for Bournemouth Corporation in 1964.

Then the variations started to appear. Walsall Corporation, well known for its highly individual approach to bus design, decided that it wanted Fleetlines, but with no front overhang and an overall length of 25ft 6in. The first was built in 1962, with its entrance behind the front axle, followed by 29 more at 27ft 6in and 69 at 28ft 6in with a narrow entrance door ahead of the front axle. Northern Counties bodied all of Walsall's short Fleetlines, and 69 of them were CRG6LW variants, with the 112bhp Gardner 6LW engine in place of the more common 6LX (and later 180bhp 6LXB). Other customers for the 6LW engine in double-deck Fleetlines were the Grimsby-Cleethorpes, Middlesbrough and Teesside municipal fleets. The only other customer for Walsall-style short Fleetlines was the SHMD Board, which in 1968 bought 10 with Northern Counties bodywork similar to that fitted to Walsall's later deliveries.

Notable deliveries to Birmingham City Transport in 1965 were 24 Fleetlines with chassis slightly longer than normal (30ft 6in) and bodied by Marshall as 37-seat single-deckers. At the time Daimler's principal single-deck model was the Roadliner, but the latter's reliability problems prompted the company formally to offer the Fleetline as a single-deck chassis, the SRG, from 1966 in 33ft SRG6LW or 36ft SRG6LX form. In practice most customers specified the 6LX engine in 33ft versions, while Leeds chose the uprated 6LXB for its 36ft examples. Independent operator Fishwick of Leyland received five SRL6-36 models with Leyland 680 engines, Northampton Corporation, the only other customer for this version, taking 20.

Also in 1966 Daimler developed a longer (33ft) version of its double-deck Fleetline, with 18ft 6in wheelbase. This model was bought initially by Leeds City Transport and went on to prove popular in municipal fleets like Belfast, Bradford, Manchester, Sheffield and Southend and with SELNEC and West Midlands PTEs. It would prove most popular, however, with customers overseas, notably in Hong Kong.

As the 1960s progressed the Fleetline customer base broadened. Deliveries during the decade peaked in 1968, in which year 540 Fleetlines entered service with British customers and the Fleetline was the best-selling double-deck chassis, outselling Leyland's Atlantean by a significant margin.

Important new customers choosing the Fleetline in the 1960s included the Birmingham and Manchester municipal fleets, which took 610 and 225 respectively, but although these orders stopped when the first Passenger Transport Executives were set up in 1969/70 the successor PTEs would continue to buy Fleetlines.

Important customers which started buying Fleetlines during the 1960s and continued into the 1970s, each taking more than 100, were the municipal fleets at Coventry (164), Derby (148), Dundee (130), Leeds (155), Nottingham (179) and Sheffield (156); among company fleets the major customers were SBG subsidiaries Alexander Midland (156), Scottish Omnibuses (102) and Western SMT (251) and BET/NBC's Northern Group (156).

Maidstone & District was a Leyland Atlantean customer right from the start, receiving one of the 1958 prototypes and buying a further 156 in the years 1959-63, but then turned to Daimler for 75 Northern Counties-bodied Fleetlines delivered between 1963 and 1968. This 1964 delivery is seen in Chatham. Tony Wilson

Left and below left: A considerable coup for Daimler was winning double-deck business from Midland Red, which had previously built the majority of its fleet. From 1963 more than 300 Alexander-bodied Fleetlines were placed in service; this 1967 example is seen in Leicester. *Tony Wilson*

Daimler FLEETLINE

NOW IN SERVICE WITH

MIDLAND RED

Yet another stage in the Fleetline success story:—
50 Daimler Fleetlines ordered by Midland Red.
These 77 seat, rear engined double deckers are already serving Midland Red on their major routes and are setting new standards in passenger comfort and operational efficiency.

UNLADEN WEIGHT 8 TONS 10 CWT.
Bodywork by Walter Alexander & Co. (Coachbuilders) Ltd.
Illustration by courtesy of Midland Red.

TRANSPORT VEHICLES (DAIMLER) LTD., G.P.O. BOX No. 29, COVENTRY.
Tel: COVENTRY 27626 (15 lines) Full technical information on request

Right: North Western was another enthusiastic BET-group convert, taking 95 Fleetlines with Alexander D-type low-height bodies between 1963 and 1967. Seen in Preston is one of 25 75-seaters delivered in 1965. Tony Wilson

Right: Trent had been a Daimler customer before World War 2 and came back in 1963 with orders for Fleetlines that would eventually total more than 100 deliveries over the next decade. This 1963 example with 77-seat Northern Counties body is seen in Derby bus station. Tony Wilson

Tynemouth & District, one of the Northern General group of companies, bought 35 Fleetlines from 1963 and later took delivery of five of the single-deck version. A 1968 delivery with 77-seat Alexander body is seen in Newcastle. Dale Tringham

Western SMT was the first Scottish Bus Group fleet to order Fleetlines in quantity and eventually bought 251, between 1965 and 1980. This 1967 Fleetline seen in Glasgow has 77-seat Alexander D-type low-height bodywork. Stewart J. Brown

The first Belfast Corporation Fleetlines were bodied in Northern Ireland by MH Cars, later renamed Potter and, when Alexander bought a majority stake in the company, Alexander (Belfast). This is the last MH Cars delivery, a 1964 CRG6LX 77-seater; the close links with Alexander are demonstrated by the rounded Alexander front end grafted on to the squarer MH body.
Howard Cunningham

Dundee Corporation had dual-sourced its fleet requirements from AEC and Daimler, but from 1964 to 1975 it standardised on Fleetlines, buying 130, including 40 33ft-long examples and 25 single-deckers. One of the 1964 deliveries, with 78-seat Alexander body, is seen in the blue livery of Dundee's successor, Tayside Regional Council. Mark Page

Although Glasgow Corporation had bought AECs, Daimlers and Leylands for some years, when it moved to rear-engined double-deckers in 1962 it went for Atlanteans in a big way. Its solitary Fleetline, with 78-seat Alexander body, was delivered in 1963 but is seen here in 1974, freshly repainted in Greater Glasgow PTE livery.
Gavin Booth

Grimsby-Cleethorpes Transport bought double- and single-deck Fleetlines in the 1960s and 1970s. This is a 1969 Roe-bodied 75-seat dual-door version.
Mark Page

SHMD Board — the Stalybridge, Hyde, Mossley & Dukinfield Transport Board, to give it its full title — had been a staunch Daimler customer in the Manchester area, often regarded as prime Leyland territory. This is a delivery from its first batch of nine, with 74-seat Northern Counties bodywork, bought in 1965. SHMD would go on to buy short-length Fleetlines, similar to Walsall's.
Dale Tringham collection

Right from the start, the Fleetline was bought by independent operators throughout Britain. In 1963 Daimler fan Burwell & District took delivery of this 73-seat Willowbrook-bodied example, seen in Cambridge.
Dale Tringham

Several Doncaster-area independents invested in Fleetlines, though this example for Premier, Stainforth, remained unique in a fleet that turned to Leyland Atlanteans and a Volvo Ailsa for its next new double-deck purchases. This bus, with a conventionally styled 78-seat Roe body, was new in 1965.
Mark Page

Several Scottish independents bought Fleetlines, including McGill's, Barrhead. Seen in Paisley, this was one of two Alexander-bodied 78-seaters bought in 1967. McGill's amassed a total of 14 Fleetlines.
Dale Tringham

Northern Counties was the first bodybuilder to tackle the slightly awkward look at the back of rear-engined double-deckers, caused by the engine compartment. On this 1967 Fleetline — the first of eight for Staffordshire independent Turner, of Brown Edge — the side profile is smooth, with faired-in corners.
Dale Tringham

Another Doncaster-area independent favouring Fleetlines — it bought four — was Felix, Hatfield. Its first Fleetline, seen here, had a dual-door 74-seat body by Roe.
Dale Tringham

Harper Bros, Heath Hayes, bought six Fleetlines, and this was one of its first pair, new in 1970 with rather plain-looking 77-seat bodywork by Northern Counties. The Harper business was sold to Midland Red in 1974 along with the Fleetlines, and two further examples on order at the time of the takeover were delivered direct to Midland Red. Dale Tringham

Yorkshire proved to be good Fleetline territory, being home to large batches operated by municipal and company operators. This 1969 Huddersfield example was one of 62 Fleetlines (including two single-deckers) bought for Corporation and Joint Omnibus Committee use; it had a 75-seat Roe body. H. J. Black

Bradford Corporation bought 95 Fleetlines — as well as Leyland Atlanteans and Titans — before being absorbed by West Yorkshire PTE. This 1968 Fleetline had 74-seat Alexander bodywork. H. J. Black

Halifax Corporation and Joint Omnibus Committee (and the JOC's short-lived successor, Calderdale JOC) bought 54 Fleetlines, including nine single-deckers. This Northern Counties-bodied 75-seater is from the first batch, bought in 1966 following evaluative trials in 1965. It wears an experimental livery for Metro, the West Yorkshire PTE, used before the standard PTE livery was designed. H. J. Black

Before being absorbed by West Yorkshire PTE Leeds City Transport bought 155 Fleetlines, including 30 single-deckers. The majority of the double-deckers were of the longer (33ft) variety, like this 1969 dual-door Roe-bodied 78-seater.
Mark Page

The hitherto independent West Riding passed into state ownership in 1967 and hence became a subsidiary of the National Bus Company. In a period of four years, from early 1968 to early 1972, it amassed 92 Fleetlines to upgrade its double-deck fleet; this 1969 example, with 76-seat Roe body, is seen in Leeds.
Mark Page

SELNEC PTE, set up in 1969, continued to buy Fleetlines and Leyland Atlanteans to the Manchester Corporation 'Mancunian' design until it evolved its own standard double-deck model. Here, in later Greater Manchester PTE days, a 33ft-long Atlantean ordered by Salford Corporation, with Metro-Cammell 78-seat dual-door body, passes a 33ft Fleetline/Roe dual-door 76-seater ordered by Manchester Corporation.
Gavin Booth

Above: Fleetlines were rare in East Anglia, though Great Yarmouth Corporation bought four, in 1963, with 76-seat Roe bodies. These followed Atlantean deliveries, and Great Yarmouth went on to buy more Atlanteans before moving to AEC Swift single-deckers. Tony Wilson

Below: Cardiff Corporation moved on to Fleetlines following deliveries of Guy Arabs, and this 1969 delivery, with dual-door 74-seat bodywork by Willowbrook, wears the later orange livery. Mark Page

Standardisation
–here now with the Daimler Fleetline

The advanced concept and well proven design of the Fleetline double decker has now been extended into single deck versions which

Gardner 6LX engine.

offer the operator a complete range of vehicles for all types of use. Double deck chassis are available with 30 ft. and 33ft. overall lengths and single

deck versions with 33 ft. and 36 ft. overall lengths.

All Fleetline single and double deck chassis have standardised main

Daimler epicyclic gearbox with right angle drive.

running units and common auxiliary components throughout.

The standard main units are the Gardner 6LX engine with 6LW and 6LXB alternatives; the Daimler epicyclic gearbox with right angle drive, and the dropped-centre drive axle.

Standard too are the Fleetline features of flat floors, and low step-free entrance ahead of the front wheels with driver controlled doors — ideal for one man operation purposes. In every case central exits can be fitted if required.

Dropped-centre drive axle.

Whether you are already a Fleetline operator, or are still considering the prospect of Standardisation, let us send you full technical specifications.

Daimler

**DAIMLER TRANSPORT VEHICLES LTD.,
COVENTRY, ENGLAND.**
Tel: Coventry 27626 (15 lines)

Right: Daimler's SRG6LX-36 demonstrator was SDU 930G with dual-door 45-seat Alexander W-type body, new in 1968. It is seen after sale to AA, Ayr. Mark Page

Right: Huddersfield Corporation was an early customer for the SRG6LX-33 model, taking two of these Roe-bodied dual-door 44-seaters in 1968.
H. J. Black

Above: Daimler was quick to promote its single-deck Fleetline chassis as a step towards standardisation. Making the point in this 1968 trade-press advertisement are Roe-bodied buses from the Leeds and Grimsby-Cleethorpes fleets.
Author's collection

Right: The first single-deck Fleetlines were the 24 double-deck chassis with Marshall 37-seat bodies delivered to Birmingham City Transport in 1965, one of which is seen here in West Midlands PTE days. Unlike the 'real' single-deck Fleetline SRG6 models that followed from 1966 they had engine 'bustles' at the rear. Mark Page

All change for Daimler?

Major changes to the structure and ownership of British bus operators at the end of the 1960s affected the Fleetline as they affected every bus manufacturer. There had been changes too in Daimler's ownership that would in time affect the future of the Fleetline range.

First the changes to Daimler. As we have seen, Daimler had been bought by Jaguar Cars in 1960, just months before the Fleetline was launched, to be joined by Guy the following year. In 1966 Jaguar merged with the ailing British Motor Corporation to form British Motor Holdings, and BMH was itself merged with the Leyland Motor Corporation in 1968 to create the British Leyland Motor Corporation. This meant that most of Britain's builders of heavyweight bus chassis — AEC, Bristol, Daimler, Guy and Leyland — were now in common ownership, along with the Eastern Coach Works, Park Royal and Roe body plants. Once deadly rivals now found themselves in the same group — a rather unwieldy empire that included most of Britain's ailing car makers and the bulk of its heavyweight-bus-manufacturing industry. This

near-monopoly of the bus market would have serious repercussions during the 1970s, and an immediate consequence was the end of production of British Leyland's front-engined double-deck models, which reduced the available double-deck range to three rear-engined types — the newly introduced Bristol VRT and the longer-established Daimler Fleetline and Leyland Atlantean.

The demise of front-engined models, like the AEC Regent, Routemaster and Renown, Bristol Lodekka, Daimler CV, Guy Arab and Leyland Titan, was hastened by the introduction of New Bus Grant to encourage operators to buy vehicles suitable for one-man operation — part of far-reaching legislation that brought the BET and Tilling bus groups under the new National Bus Company and set up PTEs in four major conurbations that swept up all of the local municipal fleets, many of them Fleetline customers.

It seemed reasonable to assume that the new West Midlands PTE would continue to be a good Fleetline customer, three of its constituents having bought Fleetlines — Birmingham (610),

Birmingham City Transport had started by keeping its options open, taking 10 early Atlanteans and 10 Fleetlines, but it came down firmly on the side of the Fleetline from 1963 with a batch of 100, which would be followed by substantial orders until its total Fleetline stock exceeded 600. This is a 1963 Metro-Cammell-bodied 72-seater, seen in West Midlands PTE days. Mark Page

Above: Walsall Corporation was another of the municipal bus fleets absorbed into West Midlands PTE and famously had a very distinctive — some might say quirky — approach to bus design. Its Fleetlines were specially built short-length buses, and there were 29 of these 27ft 6in-long examples with 70-seat Northern Counties bodies with the passenger door behind the front door and a much shorter front overhang. They also had Gardner 6LW rather than 6LX engines. Later, slightly longer buses had a narrow entrance door ahead of the front axle and a separate exit behind the front axle. Buses like this one were later rebuilt with a front entrance for one-man operation. Mark Page

At the other end of the spectrum, in 1968 Walsall bought this Daimler CRC6-36 with 36ft-long Northern Counties bodywork featuring two doors and two staircases. This chassis had a rear offside-mounted Cummins V6 engine. It was the only CRC6-36 built for a UK operator, and although it saw little service in Walsall it was used by various independents, like Vale Tours, Llangollen, where the appeal of the Walsall Building Society may have been less. Tony Wilson

Coventry Transport was absorbed by West Midlands PTE in 1974. Although an obvious Daimler customer, Coventry, like Birmingham, had controversially bought Leyland Atlanteans, in 1964, before settling on Fleetlines. This is a 1970 Fleetline with 72-seat Park Royal dual-door body. Before passing to WMPTE Coventry took delivery of 164 Fleetlines. Mark Page

Walsall (100), and West Bromwich (21). But SELNEC PTE, in the Greater Manchester area, absorbed fewer Fleetline customers — this was prime Leyland territory, after all. Bury had bought 36 Fleetlines, Manchester 225, Rochdale 26, Salford five, and SHMD 35. The other two PTEs had less of a Fleetline connection, majoring on Atlantean deliveries. Of the Merseyside PTE constituents, only Birkenhead had Fleetlines (9), while of the fleets absorbed by Tyneside PTE the only Fleetline customer had been South Shields (11).

When the first round of PTEs was created some of the constituent corporations had Fleetlines on order. SELNEC inherited outstanding orders from the Bury, Manchester and Rochdale municipal fleets, and the Rochdale and some of the Bury chassis were among the first buses to receive a new style of Northern Counties body, being in effect prototypes of the vast new fleet of buses bought over the next decade. Tyneside PTE received six single-deck Fleetlines that had been ordered by South Shields Corporation.

The National Bus Company would not prove to be an enthusiastic Fleetline customer. BET fleets had bought more than 600 Fleetlines in the 1960s and some, under NBC, would continue to buy Fleetlines as long as they were allowed, which turned out to be until 1972.

Well over 500 Fleetlines were delivered to NBC companies in the four years from the formation of the group at the beginning of 1969 to the end of 1972. While most were double-deckers, there were 135 SRG6 models. Fleets receiving their first and last new Fleetline double-deckers at this time were East Kent (20), Hants & Dorset (6), London Country (11) and Southdown (55), while single-deckers went to City of Oxford (1), Gateshead & District (6), Maidstone & District (30), Northern General (43), Potteries (21), Sunderland District (17), Tynemouth & District (5) and Yorkshire Traction (12). And the two former BET fleets that had stayed loyal to the Fleetline through much of the 1960s and had built up substantial fleets received their final deliveries; Midland Red received the last 103 of its 302 new Fleetlines (though it would later inherit two buses ordered by Harper Bros, of Heath Hayes), and Trent took the last 39 of its 109 Fleetlines.

But NBC had decided that the Bristol VRT with ECW body should be its standard double-decker, and the new Leyland National was the group's designated single-deck model, which in theory killed any potential sales for the single-deck Fleetline.

The Scottish Bus Group was not affected by the decisions of NBC and continued to buy Fleetlines until 1980, though in reducing quantities.

The second tranche of PTEs appeared in 1973/4. Greater Glasgow continued to buy Atlanteans, but South Yorkshire and West Yorkshire included some important Fleetline customers. Now brought together under South Yorkshire PTE, Doncaster had bought 31 Fleetlines, Rotherham 69, and Sheffield 156. The constituents of West Yorkshire PTE had also bought Fleetlines: Bradford 95, Halifax/Calderdale 54, Huddersfield 62, and Leeds 155.

Expansion of the existing PTE areas robbed Daimler of a few more Fleetline customers: Coventry (164 Fleetlines) was absorbed by West Midlands, Sunderland (39) by Tyne & Wear. But some of the municipal fleets had Fleetlines on order at the time the new PTEs were created: South Yorkshire received Fleetlines ordered by Doncaster, Rotherham and Sheffield (although a Doncaster order for 30 Fleetlines materialised as 15 Fleetlines and 15 Atlanteans), and West Yorkshire received Fleetlines ordered by Huddersfield.

Thus in a few years the creation of PTEs had potentially robbed Daimler of some 20 customers which in the years 1962-9 had between them bought more than half of the UK's Fleetlines. Add to that the 600-plus Fleetlines bought in the 1960s by BET companies, and Daimler, no longer really in charge of its destiny, was worried.

As things turned out, Daimler had no need to worry — not initially, at any rate. West Midlands would receive 1,209 Fleetlines, while SELNEC, dual-sourcing with Atlanteans, went on to take 570 Fleetlines, and its successor, Greater Manchester, a further 240, including no fewer than 90 that were allocated to Lancashire United Transport, which had become a subsidiary in 1976; as an independent LUT had previously bought 53 Fleetlines.

Merseyside would take just 50 Fleetlines, Tyneside and its successor, Tyne & Wear, 86, this latter figure including the six single-deckers ordered by South Shields. South Yorkshire would receive 163 Fleetlines, and West Yorkshire PTE 174, these figures again including the vehicles ordered by their respective constituent fleets. West Midlands aside, these were perhaps not the quantities Daimler might have hoped for, but fortunately there were new customers waiting in the wings.

When SELNEC PTE was set up in 1969 both Bury and Rochdale had Fleetlines on order, and some of these were delivered with early examples of the PTE's new standard bus body. This 1972 Fleetline was ordered by Bury and delivered with 75-seat Northern Counties bodywork. It is seen in Manchester following the renaming of the PTE in 1974. *Gavin Booth*

Among the more interesting buses that passed into SELNEC and then Greater Manchester PTE ownership were the 10 short-length Fleetlines bought by SHMD Board in 1969. These were broadly similar to Walsall Corporation's later deliveries, with dual-door 68-seat bodywork by Northern Counties.
Tony Wilson

Independent Lancashire United Transport worked increasingly closely with SELNEC PTE in the 1970s, and Greater Manchester Transport acquired control of LUT in 1976. Even before the change of ownership, LUT buses were becoming more similar to SELNEC/GMT standards. A 1974 Fleetline with 33ft Northern Counties 76-seat dual-door body is seen at Bolton when new.
Gavin Booth

Merseyside PTE inherited just nine Fleetlines, from Birkenhead Transport, and would buy only 50 new examples — 75-seat Metro-Cammell-bodied buses, in 1973, for services in its Wirral Division. The Leyland Atlantean became Merseyside's standard double-deck model. Mark Page

Tyneside PTE inherited Fleetlines from South Shields and Sunderland corporations and as Tyne & Wear PTE went on to buy 80 more in the years 1977-9. This is a 1979 Leyland FE30AGR, with 75-seat Metro-Cammell bodywork. Tony Wilson

South Shields Corporation had six SRG6LX Fleetlines on order when Tyneside PTE was formed, and these were delivered to the PTE in 1971, with Marshall 47-seat dual-door bodies.
Dale Tringham

The National Bus Company inherited large numbers of Fleetlines when it took control in 1969. This is a 1969 Fleetline delivery to Yorkshire Traction, with an unusual panoramic-window Northern Counties 75-seat body that had more than a touch of Alexander styling. The company had also bought Atlanteans in the 1960s. H. J. Black

One former BET-group company that favoured Fleetlines was City of Oxford, which bought unusual low-height dual-door buses. This Alexander-bodied 70-seater was delivered in 1971, and the company would receive more Fleetlines, with Northern Counties bodywork, in 1972 before moving on to the near-ubiquitous Bristol VRT.
Tony Wilson

The Northern General group of companies had bought both Atlantean and Fleetline double-deckers and built up the largest fleet of single-deck Fleetlines — 71, bought in 1971/2. This is a 1971 delivery to Sunderland District, with 44-seat dual-door Alexander W-type body, wearing the short-lived NBC blue livery. Mark Page

Among the later Fleetline deliveries to former BET companies were 12 ECW-bodied 74-seat CRG6LX models for Yorkshire Woollen, one of which is seen in NBC poppy red with MetroBus (West Yorkshire PTE) fleetnames. H. J. Black

When the Brighton Hove & District company was taken over by Southdown in 1969 the combined fleet had no rear-engined double-deckers; BH&D had Bristol Lodekkas, and Southdown its famous 'Queen Mary' Leyland Titans. An injection of more modern double-deckers started in 1969 with Bristol VRTs, and then Daimler Fleetlines. This is a 1971 CRL6 (Leyland engine) with dual-door 71-seat Northern Counties body. Although delivered in full pre-NBC BH&D livery, its traditional fleetnames were soon replaced by **'SOUTHDOWN-BH&D'** in corporate NBC style. Dale Tringham

More CRL6 Fleetlines were delivered in Southdown livery in 1972, with 74-seat ECW bodies. Dale Tringham

Midland Red was the largest BET-group customer for the Fleetline, and in 1976 it received two late deliveries with 74-seat ECW bodywork — buses that had been ordered by Harper Bros, Heath Hayes, before the latter was taken over. One is seen in the company of a more typical Midland Red Fleetline/Alexander, by now in the Midland Red North fleet following division of the giant Midland Red empire in 1981. Tony Wilson

The Scottish Bus Group companies became good Fleetline customers, following a brief and unhappy flirtation with the Bristol VRT. A total of 640 Fleetlines were delivered between 1963 and 1980. This is a 1975 Eastern Scottish bus, with 75-seat Eastern Coach Works bodywork. Tony Wilson

Highland Omnibuses received its first ever new double-deckers in 1978/9, 15 ECW-bodied Leyland Fleetline FE30AGR models. This is a 1978 delivery, in Highland's distinctive livery of poppy red and peacock blue. Mark Page

SBG fleets also received Fleetlines with Alexander and Northern Counties bodies. This example, with 75-seat Alexander D-type bodywork, was delivered in 1971 to Alexander (Fife), which amassed a total of 73 new Fleetlines.
Dale Tringham

When South Yorkshire PTE was set up in 1974 it assumed control of the municipal fleets at Doncaster, Rotherham and Sheffield, all of which contributed Fleetlines. In the 1960s Sheffield had bought both Atlanteans and Fleetlines, the latter including a number of impressive CRG6LX-33 models with 78-seat dual-door bodywork by Park Royal. This is a 1971 delivery, seen when new.
Tony Wilson

Between 1970 and 1978 London Transport bought no fewer than 2,646 DM/DMS-class Daimler and Leyland Fleetlines, with bodywork to London design built by Park Royal and Metro-Cammell. Pictured when new in 1974, a 68-seat Park Royal-bodied CRL6 pauses at Horse Guards while in use on the Round London Sightseeing Tour. Gavin Booth

There were minor differences between Metro-Cammell and Park Royal bodies on London's Fleetlines. This is a Metro-Cammell-bodied CRL6. Tony Wilson

The Fleetline, a successful model in all other markets, famously failed to live up to LT's high standards, and withdrawals began in 1978, even as the last new examples were being built. There have been suggestions that London's problems with Fleetlines stemmed from the inflexibility of its maintenance regime, and more than a touch of the 'not invented here' syndrome. Whatever the case, the London Fleetlines were quickly snapped up by other operators which seemed to suffer few of the problems experienced in London — and these operators included CMB and KMB in Hong Kong, and West Midlands PTE, where operating conditions are notoriously arduous.

Above: A photograph showing the unusual rear end of the Leyland B20 Fleetline, with its 'quiet pack' and turbocharged Leyland 690 engines. These are 1978 Metro-Cammell-bodied buses, that on the left experiencing mechanical problems — a not uncommon occurrence. By the time London's last Fleetlines were being delivered withdrawals had already begun. *Gavin Booth*

Below left: Many of the critics of the London Fleetlines might have been pleased to see this promotional vehicle representing London's buses, Underground and surface rail services. *Tony Wilson*

Below: In 1977 London Transport acquired seven 1965 Bournemouth Corporation Fleetlines with convertible-open-top bodywork by Weymann. They were used on the Round London Sightseeing Tour, with roofs in place in the winter months, as here at Victoria. *Tony Wilson*

The ex-Bournemouth DMO-class Fleetline/Weymanns operated without roofs in the summer, this example being seen at Victoria in the company of one of London Transport's short-lived Scania/MCW Metropolitans; LT bought 164 of these between 1975 and 1977, but withdrawal started in 1979, so their London lives were even shorter than the Fleetlines'. Tony Wilson

Created to run the former London Transport Country Area services, London Country required a substantial injection of new buses. Most double-deckers were Atlanteans, but in 1972 the company received 11 of these CRL6 Fleetlines, with 72-seat dual-door bodywork by Northern Counties, diverted from fellow NBC subsidiary Western Welsh. Tony Wilson

Export success

The first export Fleetlines were delivered to Carris, the Lisbon municipal operator, in 1967. This CRG6LX, with Carris-built 79-seat body, wears the Linha Verde livery used for the airport service. The 55 Lisbon Fleetlines were the only left-hand-drive examples built. Gavin Booth

Daimler had built up a respectable export business with its front-engined CVG models, Kowloon Motor Bus of Hong Kong being a particularly enthusiastic customer. Between 1949 and 1972 KMB placed 840 front-engined Daimlers in service, and it was reasonable to assume that it would come back for Fleetlines. However, the first export order came from a less obvious quarter, Carris, the municipal operator in the Portuguese capital, Lisbon, requiring 40 for delivery in 1967/8. The chassis were delivered in completely knocked-down (CKD) form and assembled locally by UTIC, which had supplied Lisbon's previous double-deckers, AEC Regent Vs. The Carris Fleetlines were bodied by the operator and were followed by 10 more in 1969 and a final five in 1971/2; the last 15 chassis were assembled by Daimler — the only factory-built left-hand-drive chassis. An order for a further batch of 25 Fleetlines for Carris was cancelled.

The next export customer was Johannesburg Municipal Transport, which in 1969 received 16 examples of the CRC6-36. This was a variant of the Fleetline, numbered in the same chassis series but with a Cummins engine mounted at the rear offside of the chassis; only one example was built for the UK, for Walsall. The Johannesburg buses had 85-seat bodies by Bus Bodies (SA), but JMT quickly recognised that the Cummins engines could be problematic and replaced these with General Motors V8 units.

More orders followed from South Africa, though for the standard Fleetline model. Daimler had sensibly shipped out UK-specification buses as demonstrators: in 1969 a Northern Counties-bodied bus was bought back from Halifax and sent to act as a demonstrator with the Cape Tramways group, while the following year a Park Royal-bodied 33-footer (one of a batch of 100 that had been ordered by Birmingham) was diverted from West Midlands to perform a similar role in Johannesburg, where it joined the JMT fleet.

The first order from South Africa for standard Fleetlines came from the Cape Tramways group, which in the years 1970-2 took a total of 62 for its Golden Arrow and Port Elizabeth operations;

50

This 1968 Fleetline CRG6LX was built for Halifax with Northern Counties body but was bought back by Daimler in 1969 and shipped out to South Africa as a demonstrator for Cape Tramways, which subsequently placed orders. Note that the body has been adapted for use in its new home, with extra-deep side ventilators. Mark Page

Diverted from West Midlands PTE in 1970, this CRG6LX-33, with 80-seat Park Royal body, was another Fleetline shipped to South Africa for use as a demonstrator, joining the Johannesburg fleet. Stewart J. Brown

an order for 63 more was cancelled. Johannesburg was a more enthusiastic customer, taking a further 129 Fleetlines between 1970 and 1976.

In the mid-1970s the absence of further South African orders was offset by substantial orders from Hong Kong. Kowloon Motor Bus, with a long history of operating Daimlers, received 450 Fleetlines between 1974 and 1979, and the colony's other principal operator, China Motor Bus, received 336 between 1972 and 1980. The KMB buses, all 33ft long, received bodywork built from kits supplied by Metal Sections (Metsec) and the British Aluminium Co (BACo).

China Motor Bus also took Metsec bodies on some of its 33-ftooters, but from 1975 CMB Fleetlines received bodywork, again supplied in CKD form, by Walter Alexander. CMB had already received a complete Alexander-bodied Volvo Ailsa in 1975, but the Fleetline order represented the start of a significant new business for the Scottish builder, which would go on to supply bodywork — in built-up or CKD form — for an increasing range of customers in the Far East.

The Portuguese, South African and Hong Kong deliveries added up to 1,059 chassis, representing 9% of total Fleetline production.

Johannesburg's first rear-engined Daimlers were 16 CRC6-36 models with 85-seat dual-door bodies by Bus Bodies (SA). Note the grille for the offside-mounted Cummins engine. Stewart J. Brown

Satisfied with the demonstrator, Johannesburg bought another 139 Fleetlines, with locally built bodywork; this 1974 delivery is a Bus Bodies 86-seater. Mark Lyons

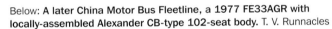

Above: A 1975 delivery to China Motor Bus, Hong Kong, which eventually bought 336 new Fleetlines; this is a 1975 CRG6-33, with dual-door 102-seat Metsec body assembled in Hong Kong from a kit. Mark Lyons

Above: The other principal operator in Hong Kong, Kowloon Motor Bus, was an even more enthusiastic Fleetline customer, buying 450 33ft-long examples. This 1977 FE33AGR has BACo (British Aluminium Co) 101-seat dual-door bodywork assembled locally from a kit. Julian Osborne

Below: A later China Motor Bus Fleetline, a 1977 FE33AGR with locally-assembled Alexander CB-type 102-seat body. T. V. Runnacles

Success in the new era

6 CHAPTER

The changes in the structure of the bus industry at the end of the 1960s that introduced Britain to the National Bus Company, PTEs and New Bus Grant happened at a time when many bus operators were rethinking the type of bus they wanted to operate. A desire to cut costs by adopting one-man operation had shifted the emphasis on to single-deck chassis in the mid-1960s; at the time OMO double-deckers were not legal. So there was a rush of new rear-engined single-deck models — Bristol's RELL, initially only for state-owned fleets, the closely related AEC Swift and Leyland Panther chassis, the unhappy Daimler Roadliner. Some fleets that had been primarily double-deck operations invested in these models in quite a big way; London Transport famously went for a large fleet of AEC Swifts, which were destined to have only short lives in London service. While some operators drifted back when OMO double-deckers were legalised from 1966, others stuck with single-deckers, further reducing the list of potential Fleetline customers.

Daimler's single-deck Fleetline proved to be a more acceptable alternative to the Roadliner for several of its customers, and its advertising made a virtue out of the possibility of a highly standardised fleet of single-deck and double-

deck Fleetlines. Indeed, most operators that bought single-deck Fleetlines also ran double-deck Fleetlines, although there were a handful — Barrow, Darlington and Northampton corporations, Gateshead & District, Sunderland District, Tyneside PTE, independent John Fiswick & Sons and the Road Transport Industry Training Board — that bought only the single-deck version. The Tyneside buses were actually ordered by South Shields Corporation before the PTE was set up.

The single-deck Fleetline was not a massive seller, but between 1965 and 1974 360 were built, the majority on 36ft-long chassis. A problem with the longer SRG models was the heavy Gardner 6LX engine perched at the end of a long rear overhang, which caused flexing and body problems.

In practice few SRG models were built after 1970, partly because British Leyland was keen to push its new integral Leyland National citybus, and to encourage sales it had other rear-engined single-deck chassis removed from the model lists.

With no front-engined double-deckers available Leyland seemed to be sitting pretty, with a monopoly of the double-deck market. If you wanted a double-decker it had to be from the Leyland stable — operators could choose a

Although Northampton Corporation had been a staunch traditional Daimler fan until 1968, it bought no Fleetlines until 1972/3, when it took delivery of 20 SRL6-36 models with 45-seat dual-door bodywork by Willowbrook. One is seen here, along with several of the Roe-bodied CVG6 double-deckers that characterised the fleet for many years. Mark Page

Another municipal fleet that came late to the Fleetline — and then only for the single-deck variant — was Barrow Corporation, which in 1971 received five of the SRG6LX-36 model, with 49-seat East Lancs bodywork. Mark Page

Having bought Daimler CCG5 double-deckers earlier in the decade, Darlington turned to single-deckers in the late 1960s, following a batch of Daimler Roadliners with the first of 36 Fleetlines. This SRG6LX-36, with 48-seat Roe bodywork, was one of the final batch of 12, delivered in 1972. Mark Page

In 1971 the Road Transport Industry Training Board bought two SRG6LX-36 Fleetlines with 50-seat Willowbrook bodywork, one of which is seen here in Edinburgh. Gavin Booth

Leyland Atlantean, Daimler Fleetline or Bristol VRT. The Atlantean appealed particularly to urban operators who were happy to have a full-height bus; the Fleetline and VRT were true low-height models, though many were bodied in full-height form, and of course both offered the ever-popular Gardner engine. The Atlantean PDR, by 1970 some 12 years in production, was giving some cause for concern. It was not as reliable as the Fleetline, and operators were demanding an improved version. This materialised in 1972 as the improved AN68 series, and this gave the Atlantean a new lease of life; it went on to serve in substantial numbers with several of the new PTEs, as well as several NBC fleets, and ultimately outlived both the Fleetline and the VRT.

Under British Leyland the Fleetline was offered with the option of the Leyland 680 engine, as the CRL6, broadening its appeal and

allowing Leyland to discontinue its low-height Atlantean variant, the PDR1/3, which had never offered the Fleetline much serious competition. Leyland-engined Fleetlines proved popular with a range of operators, often those with a strong Leyland tradition, including NBC companies. London Transport also went for the Leyland engine in a big way, as (perhaps more surprisingly) did West Midlands PTE.

New Bus Grant encouraged a fresh interest in double-deckers and many fleets took the opportunity of grants that rose to 50% of the cost of new buses to re-stock their fleets. The new PTEs were big customers, anxious to replace the widely varied inheritance from the former municipalities and introduce greater standardisation. West Midlands, unsurprisingly, went for the Fleetline, while SELNEC (later Greater Manchester) dual-sourced with larger orders for the Atlantean. Tyne & Wear also dual-

Some single-deck Fleetlines suffered structural problems caused by the weight of the engine on the longer rear overhang, and in 1980 Tayside had four Alexander-bodied SRG6LX-36 chassis (which had been new in 1970 as part of a batch of 25 delivered to Dundee Corporation) rebodied by Marshall and re-registered. They lasted just four years with Tayside before being sold. Gavin Booth

The last single-deck Fleetlines were delivered to a new customer, John Fishwick & Sons, of Leyland. These were SRL6-36 models with 48-seat bodies built locally by Fowler, a Fishwick associate. Not surprisingly, given its proximity to the Leyland factory, Fishwick was a staunch Leyland customer, and its Fleetlines at least had Leyland engines. Fishwick subsequently turned to the only rear-engined single-deck model now offered by Leyland, the National. Gavin Booth

sourced with the Atlantean, putting Fleetlines into areas with a Daimler tradition. Merseyside went for the Atlantean but took 50 Fleetlines in 1973. In 1970 barely 1,000 double-deckers entered service in Britain, but by 1973 that figure had more than doubled.

Although their quantities were inevitably much smaller, independent operators stayed faithful to the Fleetline, some right to the end. The clusters of independents in Ayrshire and the Doncaster area were good Fleetline customers throughout the model's life, although several bought Atlanteans as well; independents often had to fit in with the orders of larger companies in a bid to ensure punctual delivery.

But the Fleetline was facing a period of uncertainty. For a start Jaguar needed more capacity to build its XJ6 car range and decided to base this at Daimler's Radford plant in Coventry. The Fleetline had to move, and in 1973 production was switched to the Leyland plant in Lancashire. Perhaps inevitably, the switch caused delays in Fleetline production, and against the background of the industrial unrest of the winter of 1973/4 and the three-day week

chassis output slowed to a trickle; another consequence was that chassis and body production got seriously out of step, operators often suffering long delays before they received their new buses. In 1974 some 4,800 buses (many of them up to two years late) were on order for local-authority fleets, and of these 2,675 were Fleetlines. In the 1970s some 40% of Fleetline production was for London Transport, which caused resentment among other Fleetline customers — particularly when LT admitted in 1976 that the Fleetline was not totally successful in London service. Daimler allocated chassis numbers when orders were received, and these largely reflected the order in which the chassis were built and available to the bodybuilders for completion. Included in one batch of 100 chassis numbers were Fleetlines bodied and delivered between 1972 and 1976 — an indication of the after-effects of the earlier industrial and economic problems. Another consequence of the industrial problems was a shortage of Gardner engines, which prompted some operators to switch to Leyland engines to speed delivery.

West Midlands built up by far the largest PTE Fleetline fleet, more than 1,200 being received in the years 1969-79. Most had 76-seat bodywork built by Metro-Cammell or Park Royal, being typified by this 1978 Leyland FE30AGR/Metro-Cammell, seen at Birmingham International railway station beside a splendid time clock. While WMPTE was receiving Fleetlines it also took batches of Bristol VRT, Leyland Titan, MCW Metrobus and Volvo Ailsa, adopting the Metrobus as its standard once Fleetline production had ceased.
Mark Page

Greater Manchester PTE continued the SELNEC policy of dual-sourcing its double-deckers, orders being split between the Atlantean and Fleetline. Between 1974 and 1980 it received 240 Fleetlines, including 90 allocated originally to its Lancashire United subsidiary, among them this FE30AGR, with standard 75-seat Northern Counties body, delivered in 1979. Like West Midlands, GMT had an eye to the future and, having already sampled the Scania/MCW Metropolitan, bought batches of Leyland Titans and MCW Metrobuses before standardising on the Leyland Olympian.
Gavin Booth

In 1975 Fleetline chassis designations were changed from the familiar CRG6 and CRL6 variants to a new Leyland-inspired series. The CR-style designation dated back to the 1930s, when the CO range had been introduced. Now Fleetlines became FE (**Fleetline**), with designations that described first the length and then the engine type. So a nominally 30ft-long chassis with a Gardner engine, previously a CRG6LX, became an FE30AGR, and a 33ft chassis with a Leyland engine, previously a CRL6-33, an FE33ALR. More significantly, the Daimler name was dropped, the Fleetline becoming a 'Leyland' model.

Unsurprisingly, not all operators were comfortable with Leyland's monopoly of the double-deck market, and some were encouraging other manufacturers to introduce competing models. MCW, which had already seen the threat that the integral Leyland National posed to suppliers of single-deck bodywork, had collaborated with Scania to introduce the single-deck Metro-Scania in 1969. In 1973 it took the situation a stage further with the Metropolitan, a rear-engined normal-height double-decker based on Scania running units, and between 1974 and 1978 some 659 Metropolitans were delivered. All of the PTEs took some, perhaps as a protest against Leyland's monopoly, and even London Transport took 164 between 1975 and 1977 — although withdrawals started in 1979.

The other new double-deck model in 1973 was the Ailsa, a front-engined underframe using Volvo units. Like the ill-starred Guy Wulfrunian before it, the engine on the Ailsa was between the driver's cab and the front entrance, but the Volvo engine was a much more compact unit, and the model proved more popular than the Metropolitan. It too was essentially a normal-height model, just one, rather awkward low-height example being built.

All of which spurred Leyland into action. It was anxious to protect its market domination and ensure that it had the right model available for the London market, always the largest and one that was increasingly influencing the design of mainstream double-deckers following LT's move away from own-design models. Encouraged, no doubt, by the success of the Leyland National single-decker, which had been partly down to its decision to eradicate all the competing models, Leyland was minded to do something similar with double-deckers. A new advanced integral double-decker, coded B15, was known to be under development, and Leyland let it be known that it saw this bus as its all-purpose double-deck model and would phase out the Atlantean, Fleetline and VRT, starting with the Fleetline. It had successfully upgraded the Atlantean in 1972 with the AN68 series, and the VRT had a makeover in 1974, but the Fleetline had changed least since its introduction.

This in turn prompted several chassis builders to consider a Fleetline replacement, offering the same low-height capability and Gardner engine. Dennis, which had dabbled in double-deck chassis in the 1950s and '60s, developed the Dominator, and this enjoyed reasonable success with some former Fleetline customers, contributing to the remarkable resurgence of Dennis as a front-line bus builder. The other chassis aimed at Fleetline customers was the Foden NC, but production remained in single figures.

Leyland's B15, launched as the Titan, did not live up to Leyland's expectations, operators resisting its charms. There was feedback that it was far too sophisticated for many fleets, as well as unease that operators would not be able to have bodywork built by their favoured suppliers. Some that placed small orders decided to cancel these as doubts increased about its continuing production, and ultimately London Transport was by far its biggest customer — though it proved, for once, to be a successful design in London service.

In 1977 there emerged a more serious competitor, the MCW Metrobus, a complete vehicle, typically with a Gardner 6LXB engine. This too had London business in its sights, which it won, but it proved to be more attractive to a wider range of customers than did Leyland's Titan, selling to PTE, municipal, NBC and SBG fleets and winning orders from CMB and KMB in Hong Kong. The Metrobus was also available as a low-height bus, which increased its appeal to the likes of the Scottish Bus Group.

Against this background Fleetline orders were holding up well. The big orders from London Transport and West Midlands PTE were important, as was the recently won business from China Motor Bus and Kowloon Motor Bus in Hong Kong. Other PTE orders continued to come from Greater Manchester, South Yorkshire, Tyne & Wear and West Yorkshire.

The Fleetline enjoyed its best-ever sales in the 1970s, a consequence of New Bus Grant and PTE restocking. In 1973 alone deliveries exceeded 1,000 — nearly double the number in the model's best year in the 1960s — and even in the mid-1970s, after other types had appeared on the market and after Leyland had announced that the Fleetline was on its way out, roundly 800 new examples were entering service annually.

The Fleetline's sales were greatly helped by three-figure deliveries to customers like London Transport, West Midlands PTE and Kowloon Motor Bus. But sales inevitably started to dip once these big orders dried up, and once bodybuilders had caught up with orders delayed in the aftermath of the 1973/4 industrial problems. In 1979 deliveries dropped to barely 350, and by 1980 the Fleetline's last adherents were taking their final examples. These included steady customers like Greater Manchester PTE, the Bournemouth, Chester, Cleveland, Derby, Grimsby-Cleethorpes and Thamesdown municipal fleets, SBG's Midland and Western fleets and a clutch of independents — AA, South Notts, South Yorkshire Road Transport and Turner of Brown Edge.

The last Leyland Fleetline chassis was built in August 1980, this being an FE30ALR model, one of a pair for South Notts that entered service in 1981 as did the final examples for Bournemouth, Cleveland, Derby and Southend. The very last Fleetlines to enter service did so in 1982/3, these representing the tail end of an order for Cleveland Transit, which had stockpiled chassis built in 1978/9.

West Yorkshire PTE also dual-sourced, buying Atlanteans and Fleetlines (as well as a large batch of Metropolitans). Most, like this FE30AGR, new in 1978, had 76-seat Roe bodywork. H. J. Black

West Yorkshire also had a requirement for low-height buses, satisfied by Northern Counties-bodied Fleetlines such as this 1976 FE30AGR 74-seater, complete with a cheeky advertisement on the side. H. J. Black

South Yorkshire PTE inherited more than 250 Fleetlines and continued to receive examples ordered by the municipalities of Doncaster, Rotherham and Sheffield. First to arrive, in 1974/5, were 55 CRG6LXB/ECW 70-seaters that had been ordered by Sheffield and had a style of bodywork, featuring peaked domes, favoured only by SYPTE and Colchester Borough Transport.
Tony Wilson

More Fleetlines passed to South Yorkshire PTE from Doncaster-area independents acquired in its early years. This 1975 CRG6LX with 78-seat Roe body was one of five Fleetlines acquired in 1979 with the business of Store (trading as Reliance), Stainforth. Mark Page

One of the Doncaster independents that resisted the approaches of South Yorkshire PTE was Leon, of Finningley, which bought five Fleetlines between 1972 and 1980. This is its 1975 delivery, a CRL6 with 78-seat Roe body. Gavin Booth

The 'other' South Yorkshire — the independent South Yorkshire Motors (later Road Transport) — had bought Leyland Atlanteans before turning in 1973 to the Fleetline, of which it bought nine over the next six years. This is a 1973 CRL6, with 70-seat low-height body by Northern Counties.
H. J. Black

The independent York Pullman company bought four Fleetlines between early 1971 and late 1977. This CRG6LX, with 78-seat Roe body, was new in 1975.
Mark Page

In 1979 Cottrell, of Mitcheldean, took delivery of this FE33ALR/Northern Counties 83-seater for its services into Gloucester. The long-wheelbase Leyland-engined Leyland Fleetline was a rare variant, the only other customer being Southend Transport. Mark Page

A. Mayne & Son famously survived as an independent running into the centre of Manchester through municipal and PTE days. In 1976 it bought five Fleetlines — FE30AGR chassis with 78-seat Roe bodies. Unlike some other bodybuilders Roe was prepared to body small batches of similar bodies for independents, and buses like this could be found in Doncaster and other areas where independents still thrived. Gavin Booth

The A1 Service co-operative, based in Ardrossan, received a total of 37 new Fleetlines, including one of the very first, in 1961. Many were bought in small batches, and usually batches of similarly bodied Atlanteans were received at the same time. Owned by co-operative member Meney, Ardrossan, was this 1973 CRG6LXB, with 74-seat Alexander AL-type body. Tony Wilson

Graham, Paisley, favoured Fleetlines before turning to Atlanteans. One of its final pair of Fleetlines, delivered in 1976, was this CRL6, with 74-seat Alexander body. Tony Wilson

Municipal Fleetline deliveries continued throughout the 1970s until the very end of production, and although a number of the best municipal customers had been absorbed by PTEs there were still good orders to be won. There was continuity on Teesside, where Middlesbrough Corporation had been an early Fleetline customer, as would be its successors, Teesside Municipal Transport and Cleveland Transit. Between them the three operators bought more than 200 Fleetlines, while Cleveland would be the last operator to place a new Fleetline in service, in 1983. This 1979 delivery, an FE30AGR with 74-seat Northern Counties bodywork, carries pro-bus advertising. *Gavin Booth*

In the period 1969-73 Burton Corporation took 18 Fleetlines, including three single-deckers. This 1973 CRG6LX, seen after control of the fleet passed to East Staffordshire District Council, had a Nottingham-style Willowbrook body with seating for 78. *Tony Wilson*

Aberdeen Corporation favoured Fleetlines before turning to Atlanteans. In 1971 it took delivery of 20 long-wheelbase CRG6LX-33 chassis fitted with 80-seat Alexander bodywork.
Mark Page

Between 1970 and 1980 Chester received 30 Fleetlines. This is one of the last, an FE30AGR with 72-seat Northern Counties body. Tony Wilson

Chesterfield was an early customer for the Fleetline, taking four in 1962 and a further 37 in the period 1973-8. This 1973 CRL6 had 71-seat dual-door bodywork by Roe.
H. J. Black

Derby City Transport received some of the last Fleetlines, in 1980, but this FE30AGR, with 78-seat low-height Alexander AD-type body, was one of three such vehicles delivered in 1976.
Tony Wilson

Swindon Corporation had been a faithful Daimler customer for many years and, along with its successor, Thamesdown Transport, placed 54 Fleetlines in service between 1968 and 1980. This is a 1973 CRG6LX, with 74-seat Metro-Cammell body. Dale Tringham

Southend Transport took only long-wheelbase Fleetlines, like this CRL6-33 with 80-seat dual-door Northern Counties body, new in 1976. Southend had bought its first Fleetlines in 1971, and its last deliveries, in 1981, were among the very last examples built. Tony Wilson

Bournemouth bought Fleetlines in 1964/5, then switched to Leyland Atlanteans before returning to Fleetlines in 1973. It went on to buy some of the last to be built, in 1981. The later deliveries had Alexander AL-type bodies, like this 1978 FE30ALR 74-seater. Tony Wilson

Independent South Notts, of Gotham, bought 14 Fleetlines over a nine-year period from 1972. Its last two, delivered late in 1981, were the last two Fleetline chassis to be built, and this bus, an FE30ALR with 75-seat ECW body, was numerically the last, with chassis 8002356. Mark Page

The Fleetline in figures

The Fleetline was a success by any measure. It appeared to suffer from fewer faults than its contemporaries, notably the PDR-series Atlantean, and only London Transport seems to have experienced major problems — though for reasons, it is usually suggested, that had little to do with the basic design of the Fleetline. The single-deck Fleetline also had its problems, particularly in 36ft form, but proved to be a more successful package than Daimler's ill-starred Roadliner.

In 20 years no fewer than 11,747 Fleetline chassis were built at Coventry and Leyland, of which 11,729 were bodied. Of these, 11,369 were double-deckers, this total comprising 9,703 built to a nominal length of 30ft (including one chassis shortened from 33ft before bodying), 1,649 to a nominal 33ft and 17 36-footers. Single-deck Fleetlines totalled 358 — 78 33-footers (including 24 based on double-deck chassis) and 280 36-footers. There were also two non-PSVs, based on 33ft double-deck chassis. Export sales accounted for 1,059 Fleetlines, the majority (841) being 33ft-long chassis.

The top 10 customers for the Fleetline accounted for more than half of all deliveries. These were as follows:

1	London Transport	2,654
2	West Midlands PTE	1,209
3	Birmingham City Transport	610
4	Kowloon Motor Bus	450
5	SELNEC PTE	449
6	Greater Manchester PTE	361 *
7	China Motor Bus	336
8	Midland Red	304
9	Belfast Corporation	281
10	Western SMT	251

* including 90 buses allocated to Lancashire United following takeover by GMT

Closer examination of Fleetline sales figures reveals that well over half of all sales were to operators (or the successors of operators) that had previously constituted Daimler's traditional customer base — essentially the municipal and PTE fleets. Most notably, deliveries to Birmingham City Transport and the other fleets that passed to West Midlands PTE, plus orders from the PTE itself, accounted for more than 2,000 chassis, or 18% of all production. Municipal fleets that stayed out of PTE hands accounted for more than 1,500 sales, or 13%. The biggest municipal customers that were not absorbed by PTEs were Belfast (281) and Nottingham (179).

The more surprising customers were London Transport and the company fleets. LT's orders amounted to 2,654 Fleetlines — nearly a quarter of all chassis. Deliveries to BET, THC and, later, NBC fleets totalled 1,186, 10% of production, Midland Red (304), Trent (109) and Maidstone & District (105) being the main customers. Scottish Bus Group fleets accounted for another 640 (5%), Western SMT (251) and Alexander Midland (156) taking most. Twenty-six independent operators between them bought 224 Fleetlines, individual totals ranging from just one in some fleets to Lancashire United Transport's 53.

Daimler built five Fleetlines as demonstrators — double-deckers 7000 HP (Weymann body), 4559 VC (Northern Counties) and 565 CRW (Alexander) and single-deckers KKV 700G (Willowbrook) and SDU 930G (Alexander). There were also two single-deckers, with Willowbrook bus bodywork, for the Road Transport Industry Training Board and two double-deck chassis bodied by Yeates as tenders for use at race tracks by Shell-BP.

Several Fleetline chassis were never bodied. These included some with very early chassis numbers (60001/2), built in 1960 as experimental and demonstration CRD6 chassis, two CRG6LX in 1962 (one experimental and one for exhibition at motor shows), an experimental CRL8-36 (with British Leyland's new AEC-developed V8 engine) built in 1968 and a 1970 experimental CRL6-33, while a CRG6LX chassis built in 1967 was destroyed in a fire at Metro-Cammell. A further CRL6-33, exhibited as a chassis at various motor shows between 1970 and 1974, was eventually sold to Cleveland Transit, shortened to CRL6-30 specification and bodied by Northern Counties.

Above: **West Midlands PTE bought more than 1,200 Fleetlines, placing it second to London in sales terms, but on the day it was set up in 1969 it inherited more than 700 from the Birmingham, Walsall and West Bromwich municipal fleets. More than 600 came from Birmingham alone, among them this 76-seat Park Royal-bodied CRG6LX which had been new in 1967.** Mark Page

Left: **Delivered to West Bromwich shortly before the formation of West Midlands PTE was this CRG6LX with 73-seat ECW body, seen in PTE livery.** Tony Wilson

Midland Red built up a fleet of more than 300 Fleetlines, easily the largest within the National Bus Company, but nearly half passed to West Midlands when the PTE acquired the Midland Red routes in its area. Seen in PTE ownership is a former Midland Red CRG6LX with 77-seat Alexander A-type body, new in 1966.
Tony Wilson

Belfast Corporation and its successor, Citybus, bought 281 Fleetlines between 1962 and 1973. This is a 1970 CRG6LX-33 with 77-seat Alexander (Belfast) body, seen after transfer to Citybus. Paul Savage

Western SMT built up the largest total of Fleetlines in the Scottish Bus Group. Among the later examples was this FE30AGR, one of 50 delivered in 1978/9 with 75-seat low-height bodywork by Northern Counties. Tony Wilson

A handful of operators bought just one Fleetline. This was the sole example for Longstaff, Mirfield — a 1972 CRL6 with 78-seat Roe bodywork. Mark Page

Bodying the Fleetline

All of the surviving British double-deck bodybuilders bodied the Fleetline. Prototype 7000 HP had a fairly undramatic Weymann body that owed much to the early bodies on Leyland Atlanteans, and only the splendid fluted Daimler badge diverted attention from the plainness of the front end. Bodies to this general design would be built on Fleetline chassis for some years, notably by Park Royal and Metro-Cammell on the large batches for Birmingham City Transport and by Park Royal on the eight experimental Fleetlines (and 50 Atlanteans) for London Transport.

Northern Counties was next to body the Fleetline, producing a style that was still fairly plain but had a more solid and balanced appearance, and introduced a feature that was quickly adopted by other builders on rear-engined chassis — a valance that filled the gap between the top of the engine cover and the upper-deck floor, giving a smooth profile.

Northern Counties did a steady business in Fleetline bodies right through to the end, gathering the longest list of customers, though many were smaller orders. Northern Counties also catered for independent operators which typically wanted just one or two bodies — something that larger bodybuilders often regarded as something of a nuisance. A1, AA, Beckett, Blue Bus, Cottrell, Garelochhead, Harper, Leon, McGill, South Notts, South Yorkshire and Turner all received Northern Counties-bodied Fleetlines. More substantial orders came from operators like Greater

Like early Leyland Atlanteans, the first Fleetlines had somewhat uninspiring bodywork, and although pressure from operators produced some more stylish bodies, the plainer bodies remained available throughout the 1960s, as demonstrated by this CRG6LX/Roe 75-seater, supplied to Huddersfield in 1968. H. J. Black

74

A 1969 delivery to East Yorkshire, with plain-looking 68-seat bodywork by **Park Royal**. Tony Wilson

Metro-Cammell supplied straightforward bodies on its first Fleetlines and Atlanteans for Manchester Corporation but would move to trend-setting Corporation-inspired body styles like the 'Mancunian'. This is one of Manchester's first Fleetlines, a 1962 example with Metro-Cammell 76-seat body, looking slightly uncomfortable in Greater Manchester livery. Mark Page

Manchester and West Yorkshire PTEs, Walsall (for short-length buses), and Western SMT. And there was continuity from Middlesbrough, an early customer, through the different identities of Teesside Municipal Transport and Cleveland Transit, right through to the last complete Fleetlines delivered in 1983.

Sunderland Corporation bought an early Fleetline in 1962 and persuaded Roe to adapt its standard body with front and rear peaked domes, which improved the appearance of the bus. Roe otherwise built bodies similar to the Park Royal standard. Roe bodies were favoured by municipal fleets such as Derby, Doncaster, Grimsby-Cleethorpes, Huddersfield, Leeds and Rotherham, and, like Northern Counties, Roe also built small batches for independents, including those that survived in the Doncaster area.

The next builder to body the Fleetline was MH Cars of Belfast for Belfast Corporation's order for 88, delivered in 1962/3 and the first substantial order for the model. The MH Cars bodies were fairly box-like, and Bournemouth Corporation also took two bodies from the same builder in 1964. Successors to MH Cars — Potter and Alexander (Belfast) — would build later deliveries for Belfast.

Alexander at Falkirk bodied its first Fleetlines in 1963, the first 50 for Midland Red, and these carried a version of the body style Alexander had developed for Glasgow Corporation, but with flat-glass front screens. This body style, usually with curved-glass screens, would be built for a number of Fleetline customers over the next decade. Alexander also produced a low-height version of this body, the first example going to Scottish Omnibuses in 1963; this was quickly followed by similar bodies for other Scottish Bus Group companies and for BET's North Western and Potteries fleets.

The first Fleetlines bodied by East Lancs went to Warrington Corporation in 1963, plain but deep-windowed bodies.

Willowbrook built its first Fleetline in 1963, for the independent Burwell & District, and went on to build on Fleetline chassis for Coventry, Grimsby-Cleethorpes, Cardiff, Nottingham and Burton. It also built a significant number of single-deck bodies on SRG Fleetlines for a range of municipal and company customers.

A latecomer in terms of bodying Fleetlines was Eastern Coach Works, which builder's bodywork was, before 1965, available only to state-owned operators. Following a share exchange with Leyland, ECW bodies were once again generally available and attracted orders from municipal fleets like Coventry, West Bromwich and, later, Thamesdown, from NBC fleets like Southdown and Trent, and from Scottish Bus Group companies.

The two builders that bodied most Fleetlines were Metro-Cammell and Park Royal, which latterly concentrated on large orders, leaving Northern Counties and, to a lesser degree, Alexander to pick up the smaller orders. By this time there had emerged a broadly standard body design that was built, with local variations, by Metro-Cammell, Northern Counties, Park Royal and Roe, and this continued until the end of Fleetline production. Some of the PTEs had developed their own standard body specification, which was built by Northern Counties and Park Royal for Greater Manchester PTE, by Metro-Cammell and Park Royal for London Transport and West Midlands PTE (both of which dual-sourced bodywork for their substantial Fleetline deliveries), by Roe for West Yorkshire and South Yorkshire PTEs and by Metro-Cammell for South Yorkshire and Tyne & Wear PTEs. All of these builders survived to the end of Fleetline production, albeit only just in the case of Park Royal, which closed in 1980. By the end of the 1980s the list of bus bodybuilders had changed dramatically with the closure of Roe (1984), ECW (1987) and Metro-Cammell (1989), partly a result of the downturn in orders that coincided with the deregulation of local bus services.

Other builders that bodied on Fleetline chassis for British customers were Marshall and Pennine, both of which built on single-deck chassis only, and Massey, which bodied just one double-decker, for A1 Service.

Above right: **Northern Counties produced some fairly plain bodies before its 1970s standard body style emerged. This CRL6 Fleetline, with a 70-seat dual-door body, was new to Teesside in 1972.** Mark Page

Right: **Roe was prepared to adapt its standard body styles to suit customer requirements. This CRG6LX was new to South Shields Corporation in 1965, the front-end styling of its 76-seat Roe body echoing contemporary Alexander practice. It was photographed after the South Shields undertaking was absorbed by Tyneside PTE.** Tony Wilson

In the 1970s Roe built many bodies which were similar in design to bodywork produced by Metro-Cammell, Northern Counties and, in particular, Park Royal. This late-model Leyland Fleetline FE30AGR, with dual-door body seating 74, was delivered to Grimsby-Cleethorpes in 1980. Tony Wilson

With Scottish Bus Group orders in mind, Alexander produced the D type, a low-height version of its normal-height A-type body. This 75-seat version, on CRG6LX chassis, was built for Alexander (Midland) in 1967. Mark Page

Alexander also built bodywork on single-deck Fleetlines, like this 1970 SRG6LX-36, with 45-seat W-type body, for Yorkshire Traction. Mark Page

In 1971 Central SMT received 35 Fleetline CRG6LX chassis with flat-screen ECW bodywork. Destined to be its only Fleetlines, they were quickly transferred to other SBG companies. Mark Page

Later ECW-bodied Fleetlines for SBG companies had this version of the body with a BET windscreen, resulting in a more rounded appearance. This 1978 FE30AGR was built for Alexander (Northern).
Mark Page

Although the bodywork is plain, the deep windows and gently curved driver's windscreens improve the appearance of this East Lancs-bodied Fleetline CRG6LX, delivered in 1966 to Coventry Transport but photographed after control of the Coventry undertaking passed to West Midlands PTE.
Mark Page

Advances in double-deck body design are evident in these two former Rotherham Corporation Roe-bodied Fleetline CRG6LX in the South Yorkshire PTE fleet. The bus on the left is a 78-seater dating from 1967, that on the right a dual-door 74-seater new in 1971. Mark Page

The first examples of what would become a new Park Royal / Roe body style were built in 1969 on 20 CRG6LX chassis for East Kent. These 72-seaters would be the company's only new Fleetlines. Mark Page

After the Fleetline

With the Fleetline off the model lists from 1980, Fleetline customers had to look elsewhere. Some had dabbled briefly with Fleetlines and then moved on quickly to something else, but the type attracted some very faithful customers, which stuck with it right to the end.

The business that had been won in the early days of the National Bus Company was soon lost when NBC favoured the Bristol VRT as its standard double-deck model, and this would be followed in the 1980s by the Olympian, the model developed by Leyland to replace the Atlantean, Fleetline and VRT, and which would go on to be a highly successful bus, offering proper low-height capability with the choice of Gardner and Leyland (and later Cummins) engines. But NBC did relent in the 1970s by buying some Atlanteans, some going to former Fleetline customers like East Kent, Maidstone & District, Northern General, Southdown, Trent and Yorkshire Woollen.

From 1978 London Transport dual-sourced its orders, taking both the Leyland Titan and the MCW Metrobus, moving on briefly to the Leyland Olympian in the mid-1980s before route tendering spelled an end to bulk orders.

Of the PTEs, West Midlands moved wholeheartedly to the Metrobus, despite dabbling briefly with the Titan; Greater Manchester tried Metrobuses and Titans, as well as Dennis Dominators and Volvo Ailsas, before standardising on Olympians. South Yorkshire turned to Atlanteans, Ailsas and Metrobuses before coming firmly down on the side of the Dominator, while West Yorkshire also took further Atlanteans and Metrobuses before standardising on Olympians.

Northern General had been a good customer for double- and single-deck Fleetlines, and under NBC control it was able to buy some Leyland Atlanteans as well as the inevitable Bristol VRTs. New in 1972, an Atlantean PDR1A/1 Special, with 72-seat ECW bodywork, is seen painted in Tyne & Wear PTE yellow/white.
Gavin Booth

London Transport moved from the Fleetline to the Leyland Titan and MCW Metrobus as its principal double-deck models, and these enjoyed greater success in London service. An early Titan is seen being pursued by another all-Leyland integral product, the National citybus.
Gavin Booth

The Scottish Bus Group had bought Fleetlines as well as Ailsas and turned to a mix of Dominators, Metrobuses, Olympians and Volvo Citybuses.

It is interesting to consider the fleets that played the field when they had a greater choice in the 1970s and '80s. Of the 16 operators that bought the widest range of new double-deckers in this period — which includes London Transport, all of the PTEs and a handful of municipal and state-owned fleets — 12 also operated Atlanteans, and 10 VRTs, while, of the later models, Ailsas and Olympians (14 operators each), Metrobuses (12), Dominators (nine) and Metropolitans (eight) were particularly popular, suggesting that standardisation may have been less important to some than the ability to get new buses into the fleet, particularly when New Bus Grant (and perhaps the carrot of a good deal from manufacturers) was available.

Several of the remaining municipal fleets bought second-hand London Fleetlines, while others turned increasingly to single-deckers. Some of those that continued to purchase new double-deckers following their last Fleetline deliveries bought Atlanteans (Barrow, East Staffordshire, Grampian and Nottingham), while those that wanted Gardner engines turned to the Bristol VRT (Cardiff, Northampton) or the Dennis Dominator (Chester, Cleveland, East Staffordshire, Tayside, Thamesdown). The more adventurous went for

the Volvo Ailsa (Cardiff, Tayside), and many moved on to Olympians, often with Gardner engines, when the model became available.

But Gardner engines were becoming less common on new buses during the 1980s as the market became more crowded, European builders like Scania and Volvo finding increasing interest in their models. Both built their own engines, and when MCW announced in 1988 that it was ceasing bus production this further restricted the availability of Gardner-engined buses. Moreover, although the Dennis Dominator had started life as a Gardner-engined Fleetline substitute, its biggest customer, South Yorkshire PTE, specified Rolls-Royce engines.

Even Leyland, which had stuck religiously to its own engines in its bus-chassis range for more than 70 years, was persuaded to offer Gardner engines, first in the Titan (B15) and Olympian double-deckers and later in its Tiger, National and Lynx single-deck models. But ownership changes at Leyland put a stop to all that; following the Leyland Bus sell-out to Volvo in 1988, the Olympian was reworked in 1993 as a Volvo model. This was offered initially with Volvo or Cummins engines (the latter having already been introduced as a further alternative in the Leyland Olympian), and shortly after its launch Gardner announced that production of its 6LXB engine would cease, mainly because it could not be made to comply with Euro 1 engine-emission requirements.

London stuck to the original-version MCW Metrobus for its main deliveries of the model but in 1984 tried two of the simplified Mk II version, shown here. Most of London's Metrobuses and Titans had the Gardner 6LXB engine, as fitted to many of its Fleetlines. Gavin Booth

West Midlands PTE tried a handful of Leyland Titans before opting in a big way for the MCW Metrobus. This Mk II version was one of several double-deckers nationwide that were painted to promote bus travel in the run-up to deregulation. Gavin Booth

Above: Greater Manchester PTE stuck with Fleetlines until 1980 and
Leyland Atlanteans until 1984 but tried most other available models
before settling on the Leyland Olympian in the 1980s. This is a 1979
MCW Metrobus, with a standard Atlantean behind. Gavin Booth

Below: South Yorkshire PTE also tried other types before coming down
firmly on the side of the Dennis Dominator, though with Rolls-Royce
rather than Gardner engine. This Alexander RH-bodied example is going
through its paces on a test-track at a launch for customers and media.
Gavin Booth

Below: The Scottish Bus Group also tried different models, some former
Fleetline customers favouring types like the Dennis Dominator,
MCW Metrobus and Volvo Ailsa. Others turned to the Leyland Olympian,
here with Alexander RL body for Highland Scottish. Gavin Booth

Fleetlines in later life

With a strong reputation for reliability and, in most cases, a solid Gardner engine at the back, the Fleetline represented a good second-hand buy once withdrawn from service by its original owner. Offering a reasonable seating capacity and the promise of good fuel consumption, it was well suited to local-service and school-contract work.

There was a steady trade in second-hand Fleetlines from the 1970s, when the first of the 'big fleet' examples came onto the market, but there was a surge in sales in the mid-1980s, when deregulation of local bus services prompted several fleets to slim down considerably, while others were looking for good serviceable buses for competitive routes. In 1987 Greater Manchester disposed of almost 600 buses, mostly Atlanteans and Fleetlines, and these quickly found new buyers throughout Britain, Fleetlines joining fleets like Cambus, Northumbria, Strathtay and West Yorkshire PTE. West Midlands PTE Fleetlines also found ready homes.

The most famous mass disposal of Fleetlines resulted from London Transport's decision that, having taken delivery of 2,600-plus examples, it really didn't want Fleetlines, but operators, both in the UK and overseas, recognised a bargain when they saw one. London Fleetlines joined independent, municipal, PTE, NBC and SBG fleets, while many others were exported for further service in Hong Kong.

By the turn of the century the British Fleetline population was dwindling, only a few major fleets still operating the type, the youngest examples being now 20 years old. Fleetlines could still be found in the Arriva Derby, Chester, Strathtay, Thamesdown and Yellow Buses (Bournemouth) fleets, among others, but their days were numbered. The last closed-top Fleetlines in normal service with a major operator were Arriva's ex-Derby buses, which were withdrawn in 2008, and in the same year Thamesdown retired the last of its school-bus examples. However, at the time of writing Fleetlines can still be found in penny numbers in service with smaller operators, and the type is well represented among the ranks of preserved vehicles.

Greater Manchester PTE's decision to dispose of almost 600 buses in the early days of deregulation benefited many other fleets, large and small. This Northern Counties-bodied FE30AGR, new in 1977 to Greater Manchester's Lancashire United fleet, found its way to Northumbria. Gavin Booth

A former West Midlands PTE Fleetline FE30AGR/ Park Royal, new in 1978, in use 13 years later with A1 Service in Ayrshire. Tony Wilson

The former London Fleetlines were quickly snapped up by operators in the UK and overseas. Graham's, of Paisley, bought this 1973 Park Royal-bodied CRL6. Gavin Booth

West Midlands PTE bought a number of former London Transport Fleetlines, like this 1972 CRG6LXB with Metro-Cammell body, converted to single-door layout.
Gavin Booth

SBG fleets also bought former London Fleetlines. This 1975 CRL6/Metro-Cammell is seen with Western Scottish, complete with SBG-style destination box and paper stickers.
Tony Wilson

Among NBC fleets to benefit from London's cast-off Fleetlines was Wilts & Dorset; this 1977 FE30AGR/Metro-Cammell is pictured in Bournemouth, with a Yellow Buses Fleetline/Alexander in the background. Tony Wilson

Some Fleetlines survived into the corporate-livery era of the 1990s. Pictured running for Stagecoach East Midland in 1990, this FE30AGR, with Alexander AL-type body, had been new in 1977 to Tyne & Wear PTE. Tony Wilson

Essex-based dealer Ensign became well known for handling the disposal of London's Fleetlines. This CRL6/Park Royal was converted to left-hand drive in an effort to stimulate sales overseas. Tony Wilson

Ensign also converted three former London Fleetlines as 'Enterprise' double-deck coaches, with centre doorway and luxurious interior trim. Gavin Booth

Thamesdown Transport, the former Swindon municipal fleet, retained a significant number of Fleetlines for school work well into the 21st century. This 2005 line-up comprises mainly ex-Bournemouth Alexander-bodied buses, along with a few native ECW-bodied examples. Gavin Booth

This Greater Manchester Fleetline FE30AGR/Northern Counties, new to Lancashire United in 1978 as a double-decker, was cut down after a low-bridge accident for use on a Bury local service. Tony Wilson

West Midlands PTE decided to convert a 1978 Metro-Cammell-bodied Fleetline FE30AGR to single-deck form as a possible post-deregulation 'midibus', but the experiment was not successful. Tony Wilson

Evaluating the Fleetline

From the 1960s to the 1980s various operators conducted evaluative trials to determine the most suitable type of double-decker for their respective routes. In the 1960s these were carried out at the time when rear-engined buses were becoming increasingly popular but front-engined buses were still available from manufacturers. In the 1980s companies were evaluating first-generation rear-engined buses against the new-generation types that were appearing on the market. In most of these tests the Fleetline performed well and lived up to its reputation as a very fuel-efficient vehicle.

In 1965 Edinburgh Corporation tested Fleetline demonstrator 565 CRW against Leyland Atlantean and AEC Renown demonstrators and one of its own Leyland Titan PD3s. In terms of fuel consumption the Fleetline did slightly better than the Atlantean (8.25mpg against 8.2mpg), but the two front-engined types turned in better results (8.46mpg for the PD3, 8.56mpg for the Renown). Passenger views were also taken into consideration, and Edinburgh wanted to buy an equal number of Atlanteans and Fleetlines, but in the end it compromised, buying Atlanteans and more PD3s; it never did buy a Fleetline.

Later in 1965 Halifax Corporation carried out a more ambitious series of tests, comparing front-engined buses from its own fleet — an AEC Regent V, a Daimler CVG6 and a Leyland Titan PD3 — with other front-engined types — AEC Renown, AEC Routemaster, Dennis Loline and Guy Arab V — plus two different Atlanteans and a Fleetline. The CVG6 returned the best fuel consumption (9.8mpg), followed by one of the Atlanteans, the Fleetline, the Routemaster and the Renown. In spite of these results Halifax chose Dennis Lolines for its next order, to be followed by more Leyland Titan PD2s and finally some Fleetlines.

The Scottish Bus Group carried out a two-stage evaluation test in 1980/1. In the first, in which the newer Dennis Dominator, MCW Metrobus and Volvo Ailsa models were pitched against the established Fleetline, the Fleetline returned by far the best fuel consumption at 7.26mpg, the others returning between 5.8 and 6.2mpg. The Fleetline also had the best availability, at 95.6%. The second set of tests involved the Ailsa, Fleetline and Metrobus and the new Leyland Olympian; again the Fleetline returned the best fuel consumption (7.36mpg), the Olympian being the next best (6.61mpg), but the latter outscored the Fleetline in terms of availability (over 97%, compared with 95.7%). All of the newer types would figure in SBG's future orders.

Above right: The Scottish Bus Group carried out the first of two evaluative tests in 1980, comparing an Alexander Midland Fleetline/ECW (far left) with, from left, an MCW Metrobus/Alexander, a Volvo Ailsa/Alexander and a Dennis Dominator/Alexander. The Fleetline returned by far the lowest fuel consumption and enjoyed the best availability. Gavin Booth

Right: Although the Fleetline did not fare so well in the 1965 Halifax comparisons, it later became a standard model; this CRG6LX with 74-seat Northern Counties body was new in 1972 to the associated Calderdale JOC fleet. Tony Wilson

Appendices

FLEETLINE CUSTOMERS

Municipalities / JOCs

Aberdeen	44
Barrow *	5
Belfast **	281
Birkenhead	9
Birmingham **	610
Bournemouth	89
Bradford	95
Burton-on-Trent **	18
Bury **	36
Calderdale	17
Cardiff	92
Chester	30
Chesterfield	41
Cleveland	64
Coventry	164
Darlington *	36
Derby **	148
Doncaster	31
Dundee **	130
Glasgow	1
Great Yarmouth	4
Grimsby-Cleethorpes **	82
Halifax **	37
Huddersfield **	62
Leeds **	155
Manchester	225
Middlesbrough	60
Northampton *	20
Nottingham	179
Rochdale **	26
Rotherham **	69
Salford	5
Sheffield	156
SHMD	35
South Shields	11
Southend	72
Sunderland	39
Swindon	19
Teesside	86
Thamesdown	35
Walsall	100
Warrington	26
West Bromwich	21
Total	**3,465**

London Transport / PTEs

London Transport	2,654
Greater Manchester	271
Lancashire United	90
Merseyside	50
SELNEC	449
South Yorkshire	163
Tyne & Wear	80
Tyneside *	6
West Midlands	1,209
West Yorkshire	174
Total	**5,146**

BET / THC / National Bus Company

East Kent	20
East Yorkshire	35
Gateshead & District *	6
Hants & Dorset	6
Hebble	1
London Country	11
Maidstone & District **	105
Mexborough & Swinton	11
Midland Red	304
North Western	95
Northern General **	66
City of Oxford **	60
Potteries **	72
Southdown	55
Sunderland District *	17
Trent	109
Tynemouth & District **	40
Tyneside	5
West Riding	92
Yorkshire Traction **	31
Yorkshire Woollen	45
Total	**1,186**

Scottish Bus Group

Alexander (Fife)	73
Alexander (Midland)	156
Alexander (Northern)	8
Central SMT	35
Highland Omnibuses	15
Scottish Omnibuses	102
Western SMT	251
Total	**640**

CUSTOMERS FOR SINGLE-DECK FLEETLINES

Barrow Corporation	5
Belfast Corporation *	30
Birmingham City Transport	24
Burton-on-Trent Corporation	3
Bury Corporation	9
Darlington Corporation **	36
Derby Corporation	5
Dundee Corporation *	25
Fishwick, Leyland *	5
Gateshead & District *	6
Grimsby-Cleethorpes Transport	4
Halifax Corporation	9
Huddersfield Corporation	2
Leeds City Transport *	30
Maidstone & District *	30
Northern General *	43
Northampton Corporation *	20
City of Oxford *	1
Potteries *	21
Rochdale Corporation	4
Rotherham Corporation	2
RTITB *	2
Shell-BP ***	2
Sunderland District *	17
Tynemouth & District *	5
Tyneside PTE *	6
Yorkshire Traction **	12
Daimler (demonstrators) **	2
Total	**360**

* 36ft models only
** 33ft and 36ft models
*** Non-PSV, based on double-deck chassis

CUSTOMERS FOR 33ft DOUBLE-DECK FLEETLINES

Aberdeen Corporation	20
Belfast Corporation	70
Bradford City Transport	40
China Motor Bus	305
Cottrell, Mitcheldean	1
Dundee Corporation	40
Johannesburg Municipal Transport	102
Kowloon Motor Bus *	450
Lancashire United Transport	26
Leeds City Transport	100
Manchester City Transport	47
SELNEC PTE	198
Sheffield Transport	30
Southdown	25
Southend Corporation Transport *	72
West Midlands PTE	132
Western SMT	7
Total	**1,665**

Independents

AA, Ayr	12
A1, Ardrossan	37
Beckett, Bucknall	1
Blue Bus Services (Tailby & George), Willington	5
Blue Ensign, Doncaster	3
Blue Line (Morgan), Armthorpe	5
Burwell & District	2
Cottrell, Mitcheldean	2
Felix, Hatfield	4
Fishwick, Leyland *	5
Garelochhead Coach Services	3
Graham, Paisley	15
Harper Bros, Heath Hayes	6
Lancashire United Transport	53
Leon, Finningley	5
Longstaff, Mirfield	1
Mayne, Manchester	5
McGill, Barrhead	14
Premier (Wilson), Stainforth	1
Procter, Hanley	2
Reliance (Store), Stainforth	5
Rossie Motors, Rossington	3
South Notts, Gotham	14
South Yorkshire, Pontefract	9
Turner, Brown Edge	8
York Pullman	4
Total	**224**

Miscellaneous

Daimler (demonstrators) **	5
RTITB (training buses) *	2
Shell-BP (race-track tenders)	2
Total	**9**

Export

Carris, Lisbon	55
Cape Tramways Group	62
China Motor Bus	336
Johannesburg Municipal Transport	156
Kowloon Motor Bus	450
Total	**1,059**

* Single-deck Fleetlines only
** Single- and double-deck Fleetlines

Bibliography

British Double Deckers since 1942
    by A. A. Townsin (Ian Allan, 1965)
Daimler by Alan Townsin (Ian Allan, 2000)
Daimler Rear-Engined Buses by Stewart J.
    Brown (Bus Enthusiast Publishing, 1985)
*The Best of British Buses, No.11: Post-war
    Daimlers 1942-1981* by Alan Townsin
    (Transport Publishing Company, 1986)

Between 1972 and 1981 South Notts, the Gotham-based independent, received 14 Fleetlines, including the two last chassis built. These are earlier South Notts Fleetlines at Loughborough in 1978 — both CRL6 models with 75-seat Northern Counties bodywork, and dating from 1972 and 1975. All South Notts Fleetlines were Leyland-engined, and all but the final pair had Northern Counties bodies. Gavin Booth